A PRACTICAL
STRATEGIC

WORDS

THAT GET

RESULTS

FELIPE MORENO

WORDS THAT GET RESULTS

TABLE OF CONTENTS

PART II: THE CASES

PART III: THE MATERIAL

INTRODUCTION

D o you find it hard to express yourself clearly? Have you ever felt your ideas lose their impact when you say them out loud? This may have happened during a presentation, in a work meeting or when texting your partner—or boss. If so, you're not alone.

Mastering communication isn't easy. The value of human connection has never been more crucial (it sets us apart from artificial intelligence.) And yet, the relentless pace of change leaves little room for error. A single misstep and you miss the mark. In this challenging scenario, effective communication becomes paramount.

This book is a roadmap to honing this vital skill by mastering the art of strategic messaging.

Part art and part science, strategic messaging is a subtle craft. It's about using language to inspire and mobilize action. It allows you to turn strategic insights into words that get results.

More than a theoretical exploration, this book is a practical guide. It offers a step-by-step method that is easy to understand and apply in real life: by the end of these pages, you'll add crafting and delivering strategic messages to your skill set.

The method & the model

The content is organized around the method. The five central chapters correspond to the method's five steps, which include planning, building, structuring, calibrating and executing. Each chapter focuses on a primary procedure, delving into the related ideas and providing conceptual context to technical principles and tools. The book is also full of practical examples and real-life cases, which show how the method works in practice by relating it to everyday experience.

Strategic messages are clear and concise. They are memorable phrases with the potential to mobilize people around your goals, resulting from careful analysis. Their effectiveness depends on pragmatic reflections and adding in variables such as who the audience is, what your outcome should be, or how much credibility you have. The resulting clarity and relevance make these messages meaningful to your strategic arsenal.

While all this may sound familiar, this book offers a unique approach. Most strategic communication proceedings have the same shortcomings: they don't go deep into the message. It's far more common to find general guidelines or menial tips on what to do but not much about what to *actually say*.

This method is a practical guide for applying the technical Strategic Messaging Model (SMM©) that I created and codified. Together, they do something akin to language engineering, using logic-linguistic principles in the same way that engineering uses mathematical rules. This approach allows us to put strategic insights into words. Concrete, specific words that become subjects, verbs, and complements. This is achieved through the linguistic SMM© equation, a formula for producing strategic messages.

When executed thoroughly, this equation consistently yields a message of strategic ascendancy. It is usually 6-12 words long and has a 75% success rate of achieving the intended goal.

We know this because we've measured it hundreds of times. My team and I have worked with over 5,000 individuals and 70 organizations. These include multinationals across a range of sectors and industries: IBM, Walmart, Pfizer, BHP, Scotiabank, BBVA, Danone, ORICA, Banco Santander, Kuehne+Nagel, and TEVA. We've also worked with local companies that have gone global, ranging from commodities to luxury outdoor tourism. We've worked with the copper mining giant CODELCO and the inspiring Explora Hotels.[1] We've also worked with LATAM Airlines Group, CMPC, Falabella, and VSPT Wine Group. Trade associations, government ministries, central banks, and universities have also hired us.

We've used the SMM© model in the "pure" form you're about to learn and as part of corporate narratives and communication strategies. Easy tailoring to specific needs and situations is proof of the model's high flexibility and applicability, which delivers optimal results in different industries and sectors.

Before starting my own business, I built a career as a consultant. I helped companies and leaders with their strategic and communications challenges. Before that, I worked in political communication. I was the lead speechwriter for the Chilean Minister of the Interior. I moved to politics after six years in a corporate marketing job in London.

Many of the examples in the book are from business, politics, and communications, the work environments I've become familiar with. However, there are many more areas where good messaging is vital. So, you will likely find an almost immediate use for the book if you're a businessman, manager, politician, or entrepreneur. The same goes for experts, independent consultants and professionals. Especially if the job involves leadership or teaching.

---

1 The hotel has been awarded the World's Leading Expedition Company by the World Travel Awards (www.worldtravelawards.com.) It has won five consecutive years (2019-2023.)

And if you're not dedicated to one of the listed areas, don't worry, strategic messaging is valuable to everyone regardless of their role or profession. It can be helpful at work, school, home, the field, and on the street. Even if you're a solitary artist, a grumpy writer, or a music diva, you still need to interact with others. It could be with your editor, agent or whoever stands for you.

Our social nature vs. the AI menace

British evolutionary psychologist Robin Dunbar found that our brains are social by nature, becoming large and complex to navigate our complex social systems.[2] That's why psychotherapist Virginia Satir said people's well-being relates to communication. Well-being depends on social interactions, she reckoned. And communication is "the lifeblood of relationships."[3]

In the last decades, interpersonal human skills have become highly valued. Known as "soft," "durable," or "life" skills, they are distinctive human abilities. As such, they usually involve working with people. They are applicable in all areas of life but especially at the workplace, where they have become precious. Communication generally ranks above them all.

There are two main reasons for this. First, human communication has a dual purpose. On the one hand, it's a skill in itself. However, it also enables similar vital skills, such as teamwork, leadership, and conflict resolution.

Investor Warren Buffett says that communication is one of the easiest ways to get ahead. "You can have all the brainpower in the world, but you must be able to transmit it. And the transmission is communication."[4] A study of 80 million job ads between 2019 and 2020 across 22 US industries backs up Buffett's advice. Seven of the top ten skills employers look for

---

2 Dunbar, 1998.
3 Suárez, 2004.
4 CNBC, 2018.

are soft skills. Of those seven, communication consistently ranks in the top five.[5]

The second factor that has raised the value of human communication is AI. It can handle most tasks, with robots replacing people. This will happen in most activities and sectors. The exceptions will be those that rely on human interaction.

Intuition, empathy, and social and emotional intelligence are central to human connection. They enable us to read hidden signals and unspoken cues. It helps us understand other people's feelings and adapt to always-shifting social dynamics. These subtleties present an almost insurmountable challenge for AI, at least for now.

Moreover, as AI takes over, humans will cluster on the areas where they are less replaceable. This will probably be at the top or beginning (and end) of value chains. Most middlemen will be robots, while creators and consumers will remain human.

In addition, today's companies are becoming more horizontal, flexible, and competitive. This requires leaders who can persuade other humans, not just write prompts. They must align diverse interests and mobilize others towards shared goals. And last but not least, they must also inspire their teams with meaning and purpose.

But doing this today is challenging. Modern urban life is saturated with stimuli and distractions, from street neon signs to the bedtime smartphone roll. Thus, there is enormous pressure for communication to be shorter and more straightforward. This is much easier to consume than to produce—almost inversely proportional. The shorter and more concise the message (while retaining its meaning,) the longer it takes to make.

This need for immediacy and brevity has led to an unprecedented use of images. They are now ubiquitous. In fact, it is often said that "a picture is

---

5 America Succeeds, 2021.

worth a thousand words." The phrase seems to encapsulate a self-evident truth. It's common knowledge among advertising and salespeople that images help you sell. But usually, this comparison is between an ad having an image and the same ad not having an image. However, the issue is not between an ad having only an image versus having only text. Those comparisons are unusual as text and images use different channels. Traditionally, this has meant different formats, supports, and materialities. Until now.

Of bits and bytes

Digitization has reduced text, images, and sound to bits. This reduction is astounding, almost magical. Think about the *Encyclopaedia Britannica* in physical vs. digital when you move to a new home. In fact, we have come to contrast "digital" with "physical" in colloquial speech. But the truth is that bits have materiality. They are not made of ether or ectoplasm. They are processed and stored. They need electricity and are measured in bytes which can work as an objective metric for both words and images. Therefore, it enables us to measure their actual cost and check whether it's true that a picture is worth a thousand words.

If we consider social impact and cultural influence as a measure of value, the phrase does not necessarily hold true. Books like *The Bible*, Marx's *The Capital*, Homer's *Iliad*, or Adam Smith's *The Wealth of Nations* can take up 1 million bytes (1 MB) each.

In contrast, a good quality photo taken by a smartphone or digital camera weighs about 5 MB in JPG format and 25 MB in RAW format (higher quality.) Most pictures that usually rank among the most influential are photojournalism like Nick Utt's *War Terror*, Dorotea Lange's *Emigrant Mother*, or Jeff Widener's Loyal *Tank Man*. The cost in bytes for any of them is between double and five times that of the aforementioned books.

In 2017, Pepsi released a cheeky Halloween ad of a can of Pepsi wearing a Coca-Cola cape. The message was only 6 words: "We wish you a scary Halloween," poking fun at its rival. Coca-Cola's response was not long in coming. Keeping up a message of only six words, it said "Everyone wants to be a hero," mocking Pepsi. Both ads used the exact same image. They both share a tagline of 6 words. Those 6 words made the difference on the meaning.

The reason for this is words' outstanding capacity to harness meaning. When used properly, they can be superb communication tools. Effective and efficient. Short, clear, and concise.

This is far from what schools and universities taught many of us. Even today, in secondary school and higher education, we still tend to write long texts. These can be essays of 1,000 words or more, or dissertations and theses of over 15,000 words. In the workplace, however, we need to be able to write shorter and more polished pieces of work. A resume or cover letter is the most extended item most people have to write. This is under 300 words.

As a result, the most common mistake in presentations, meetings, or emails is to include too much information. Too many slides, words, and pictures. This is risky, as audiences lose interest at the first sight of repetitive or irrelevant content.

Companies waste money training executives to present or negotiate. Both skills require clear messages. Keeping it simple is a prerequisite and an earlier, more fundamental skill.

Confusing messages undermine the clarity of the speech. They compromise communication's effectiveness and make it difficult to succeed. They also make the speaker look untrustworthy. This can affect the way work is done and the relationships between teams.

Messaging & leadership

In fact, one of the most crucial tasks leaders are faced with is to communicate the company's strategy. To do this, they should be clear and precise. "Without clarity, there is no direction," said strategy expert Eric Van Steen.[6] Leaders must also set things in motion or align courses of action toward the strategy. They do so by "getting things done through others." This is what persuasion expert Robert Cialdini insightfully called it. It is one of the most essential leadership skills.[7]

This places a threefold demand on their messaging. Leaders must be able to build and deliver a message that is clear, relevant, and true. It's a challenging task, especially without training. This is why messaging is becoming so important. It benefits both the individual and the organization.

This book is easy to read as a technical guide, covering the method step by step in the book's first section. The second section presents four real cases fully developed through the five steps of the method. You will also find additional resources in the third section of the book, in the form of a glossary of terms and a five-page instruction manual as appendices.

The SMM© model is a pragmatic synthesis of several disciplines: linguistics, strategy, rhetoric, and philosophy of language. This consolidation was then enriched with practical techniques I learned in the communications industry.

Today, most of our work comes from repeat clients and word-of-mouth. This is mainly due to the ease and speed with which our clients can adopt the SMM©, who quickly understand its value and applicability. Managers and executives with engineering or science backgrounds particularly appreciate the model. It's in tune with their

---

6 Van Steen, 2021.
7 Cialdini, 2001.

technical nature and helps them to articulate effective messages without relying on talent or improvisation.

All examples and cases in the book are genuine. Sensitive details, names and events have been modified; however, I've cared to ensure each situation represents what happened.

PART I:

THE MODEL AND ITS METHOD

STRATEGIC MESSAGING MODEL

STEPS

> **Think and plan:** Context, audience, ethos, goal and outcome.

> **Find the hinges:** Target action and key motivation.

> **Do the magic:** Build the message through the SMM© equation.

> **Bring that support:** Calibrate evidence and ethos.

> **Making it real:** Prepare the execution.

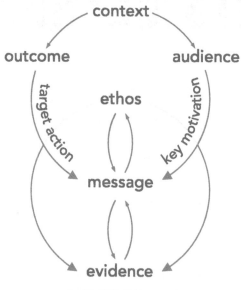

THINK FIRST, THEN PLAN

This chapter delves into the concept of strategy, emphasizing the importance of strategic planning in communication. First, the model starts with the philosophical underpinnings of our understanding of reality. They influence our strategic thinking, but especially our notion of context. Then, it introduces four key elements: context, audience, ethos, and outcome. It goes through each factor, examining its inner workings and practical applications. The chapter also shows their interconnectedness, how their interplay is dynamic and how they can be leveraged to achieve communication outcomes.

In the beginning, it was not the word but strategy. Although this book is about messaging, the SMM© anchors in that subtle realm. The wording comes later. Thus, the first and most important thing at this stage is to forget what you want to say. Forget about whatever message you have invented. Let's start with strategic definitions. They can work, in fact, as strategic variables and components. What do I want to achieve? Who do I want to address? What is the context? How much credibility do I have? The answers to these and other questions will work together. They will advance your strategy by using them as persuasive drivers.

But what is strategy, anyway? In general terms, strategy is a broad plan that helps achieve relevant goals. It also involves a context of uncertainty. If not, you are talking more about a process or method.

Dealing with the primal uncertainty of experience is part of the human endeavor. We cope with it through expectation and planning. The term strategy finds its origins in the realm of warfare. This is because war has high stakes. It's one of the human activities most prone to going wrong. And, as in love, there are no rules.

The English word comes from the Greek term *strategikà*. It evolved from *strategòs*, the name of the top general of a land-based army in Ancient Greece. Add the Greek suffix "*kà*" to make a word plural. It means "all things related to." *Strategikà* is "all things related to the top general of a land-based army."

STEPS:

1. Think first, then plan:
   context, audience, ethos and outcome.

2. Find the hinges: target action and key motivation.

3. Do the magic: build the message through an equation.

4. Bring that support: calibrate evidence and ethos.

5. Making it real: prepare the execution.

1.1. Mind the context

One of the keys to strategic thinking is understanding context. However, defining context is elusive, as it encompasses the vast external landscape that influences your strategy. It's a tapestry of circumstances and factors that shape both how you carry it out and its outcome. As you may suspect, those circumstances and factors aren't set. They are different in every case.

For centuries, Western philosophy has embraced the idea of an objective, clear reality. This view began with Plato and went through Christianity and the Enlightenment to peak with Kant. However, a different viewpoint has gained traction recently. It emphasizes chaos and uncertainty as fundamental to existence. This is the "B-punk" side of philosophy that goes back to Heraclitus' analogy of life as a river. It challenges the idea of a fixed, knowable reality. It holds a view that embraces chaos and uncertainty as the very essence of our existence.

Heraclitus famously compared existence to a flowing river. Because, similar to what happens with the waters in a river, nothing remains the same in our lives. Everything is interconnected and in permanent transformation.

This ever-changing mixture is the habitat of life. The "dark placenta of becoming," as Nietzsche would later call it. In this relentless flow of constant change, things became hard to grasp. "You cannot step into the same river twice," Heraclitus said. Nietzsche would even say it exists in this vortex of "becoming."[8] Therefore, their essence is beyond the scope of our knowledge.

With the advent of Modernity, this perspective has become mainstream. Marshall Berman describes the essence of this era in his book *All That Is Solid Melts into Air*. For him, being modern combines human potential and existential angst. Modernity promises "adventure, power, joy, growth, transformation of ourselves and the world." But it

---

8 Scruton, 1996.

also threatens to "destroy everything we've been, everything we know, everything we are." [9]

Berman published his groundbreaking book in 1982. That same year, *Time* magazine named the computer Machine of the Year.[10] It also coincided with the arrival of the first personal computer, the IBM 5150, just a year earlier.

These events were important milestones in an ongoing technological transformation. Subtle at first, these technologies would eventually move several traditional industries into an information-based economy, which would come to be known as the Third Industrial Revolution. Also known as the Information Age, the economic shift was primarily driven by the 'dematerialization' of goods and services through digitalization, which had a big impact on information-heavy industries like finance and media.

Vaclav Smil put this in perspective in his 2022 book *How the World Really Works*. The world has changed remarkably in the 80 years after World War II (1945-2020).

We have achieved unparalleled well-being standards for the human population never seen in history. For the last three generations, geopolitics expert Peter Zeihan says, "it has been a period where everything has been getting faster, better, and cheaper."[11]

Yet, in strict material terms, the transformations weren't as dramatic as they seemed. More fundamental were the changes experienced before World War I (1834-1914). Smil asserts that we will not relocate to Mars or eat crops grown in skyscrapers. We will keep getting our food from agricultural farmland and our energy from oil. [12]

---

9 Berman, 1983.
10 Time, 1982.
11 Zeihan, 2022.
12 Smil, 2022.

However, digitalization has undeniably accelerated the production, transaction, and consumption of "dematerialized" products. It produced a soaring growth of digital products and fueled the rapid growth, transnational reach, and cultural influence of both the financial industry and the media.

This ever-increasing volume and pace of digital realities democratized a new anguish. It's the feeling of living in an uncertain world. This was traditionally a privilege of postmodern scholars, tormented intellectuals, and pretentious artists. Now, almost every average Joe can experience this feeling. Zygmunt Bauman's concept of "liquid modernity" encapsulates this experience, echoing the fluidity and unpredictability of Heraclitus' river in contemporary life.

The idea extended beyond sociology. Academia and business circles have been using VUCA to describe today's world. The acronym (Volatility, Uncertainty, Complexity, and Ambiguity) reflects our unpredictable and intricate times. Although still in use, VUCA was recently contested by a new acronym: BANI. It stands for Brittle, Anxious, Nonlinear, and Incomprehensible. This new acronym highlights the fragility, anxiety, and inherent nonlinearity we face.

This fluid reality is interwoven with our personal stories and collective narratives. In his book *Sapiens*, Yuval Harari exposed the extent to which we are story-driven animals.[13] Drawn to believe our fiction, we've created stories and internalized them as truths. Although this can be seen as a liability at first sight, it is the source of our main evolutionary advantages.[14]

---

13 Harari, 2008.

14 Traditionally, human beings' evolutionary advantage has been described from an individual point of view (rational animal, etc.). However, Harari remarkably shows us that the main advantage is collective. We're the only species in the animal kingdom that can cooperate in large numbers and in a flexible fashion. Ants or bees can cooperate in large numbers. But when faced with a hose, they cannot reorganize and save their queen from flooding. Some animals can cooperate flexibly. But they do so in small, reduced groups. They only cooperate with those they have groomed for a long time. Using

Harari calls the products of these fictions "imaginary orders." They include concepts like God, money, human rights, religions, ideologies, and national identities. These imaginary orders are a vital part of our evolutionary advantage. Belief in these shared fictions lets Homo sapiens cooperate flexibly. They did so in large groups. This ability has been a weapon of mass destruction in assuring our dominance as a species.

The orders overlap between them and with our individual biases and collective narratives.

Context is about more than just the immediate surroundings. It's a complex web of factors that significantly influence meaning. Imagine context as a tapestry. Its threads range from long-standing cultural values to the audience's mood. Sometimes, the venue's layout or distribution of chairs can make a difference.

The term itself reflects this complexity. "Context" comes from the Latin *contextus*, meaning "a joining together, scheme, or structure." But its original meaning, "to weave together," paints a more vivid picture. When someone is taken out of context, it implies removing their intended meaning. It was ripped from the tapestry. It's not what they meant.

The degree of influence determines what qualifies as context. The natural sciences have a decisive say in the physical world. They describe, understand, and predict natural phenomena based on cold, hard evidence product of meticulous observation and experimentation.

This approach would be enough if we were all Tom Hanks in *Cast Away*, stranded on a deserted island. But most of us live in a world crowded with other people. It's the hell of "others," as Jean-Paul Sartre so parisianly described. The problem is that human behavior is complex, and

---

Harari's example, imagine what would happen if we put 50,000 chimpanzees in Wembley Stadium. However, humans can cooperate well, and can do so in huge groups. In fact, what makes us cooperate large and flexibly is precisely our ability to believe our own fiction.

so is our decision-making. Many factors can influence it, including past experiences, cognitive biases, age, socioeconomic status, and core values. Belief in personal relevance also matters.

This is where the social sciences step in (the humanities and the arts can also help.) Among them, behavioral sciences have gained prominence. A compound of anthropology, psychology, and sociology, it has a practical, empirical approach. In his book *Behavioural Insights*, Michael Hallsworth summarizes the main findings. Much of our behavior is nonconscious, habitual, and driven by environmental cues.[15]

Following the work of Nobel winner Daniel Kahneman, Hallsworth reinforced the two-brains thesis. "There are two main ways of thinking that influence our behavior," he stated. One is controlled, slow, deliberative, reflexive and self-aware. The other is uncontrolled, fast, intuitive, and unconscious. Due to this, the way choices are presented, framed, and positioned is much more relevant than we're aware of.

As we've seen before, thinkers like Nietzsche, Berman, Smil, Bauman, and Harari agree. Our reality is a relentless flux in permanent change, and that reality is influenced by humans and their behavior, which is also hard to predict. The main challenge is finding the proper focus to determine what are the most relevant factors and conditions in the given context. Otherwise, the sheer complexity of our experience may become overwhelming and paralyzing.

Moreover, the challenge is also how to deal with a dynamic and casuistic reality such as context? How to detect patterns within context that could work as input for strategic analysis.

After several iterations and trial and error, my team and I discovered that the best way to address a dynamic reality was with a model that integrates that dynamism.

---

15 Hallsworth, 2020.

The SMM© here helps disentangle the causal relationships behind actions and situations. It's a tool for identifying those that have strategic value. Then, it serves as a road map, indicating where we are going and how we intend to get there. This results from the combined, integrated action of four parts: goal, audience, ethos, and facts (see Figure 2.)

In the method outlined in this book, the first step in devising a strategy involves a crucial analysis of context. The model presented here aids in unraveling the causal relationships behind actions and situations, identifying those with strategic value. This serves as a roadmap, guiding our direction and approach.

Formulated through questions, these would be the responses to what my goal is. Who is my audience? How much credibility (ethos) do I have? What are the facts?

These elements, when combined and integrated within a specific communication act of a real strategic challenge, make all the difference. By understanding and leveraging context, we can navigate the complexities of our world and make informed decisions that lead to effective action.

Figure 2

1.2. Define an outcome that serves your goal

Causality is at the core of human inventiveness. It's the backbone of any successful plan. Without understanding causal relationships, your plan is destined to fail. These relationships exist throughout the world, both natural and human made. A cause, which we can call phenomenon A, influences another, phenomenon B, the effect. Uncovering these relationships is the very purpose of science. It ranges from physics and chemistry to economics and anthropology.[16]

Causality links human purposes with actions. It hones our ability to foresee the future and make plans. This is a crucial skill for using context strategically. This planning requires understanding human nature and how the world works. As people's behavior impacts how things develop, their motivations and perspectives matter. Each person's actions converge towards their outcomes, needs, and intentions.

This is precisely why strategists are typically senior-level people, experienced or streetwise. They frequently hold leadership positions or have significant power. Why? Because a well-crafted strategy allows you to achieve your goals. And achieving goals nurtures your power. As Sun Tzu famously stated in his timeless treatise on strategy, The Art of War: "What enables the wise sovereign and the good general to strike and conquer and achieve things beyond the reach of ordinary men is foreknowledge."[17]

In his best-selling book The 48 Laws of Power, Robert Green delves into what is required to play the game of power. He emphasized that one of the most important things is to distance oneself from the present. Then, consider the future objectively and strategically. As Green says, "The further you see, the more steps ahead you plan, the more powerful you

16 Hunt, 2008.
17 McCreadie, 2018.

become."[18] This is why chess, with its calculation of future moves, has become the symbol of strategy.

Innovation consultant Max McKeown echoes this view. He defined strategy as "the ability to get desirable ends with available means."[19] This captures a fundamental aspect of being strategic. It involves actions that have an impact. These actions modify a given state of affairs into a more beneficial or less harmful one.

The other key feature is its ability to instrumentalize for the greater good. This means viewing situations, facts, and objectives as tools to achieve a larger goal. It also includes people acting for our benefit, sometimes even against their interests. In most cases, they do so because, somehow, they have been cheated or deceived. This brings us to the third essential skill for strategically leveraging causality: master the art of managing appearances. This is especially true in competitive scenarios, where it is key to limit the opponent's ability to predict your moves.

Skilled chess players can gain an edge by disguising their intentions. It can be a powerful, complementary tool beyond the sole calculation of moves. Moreover, strategic thinkers excel at integrating seemingly opposing ideas. Losing a battle to win the war. Or sacrificing a short-term gain for a long-term benefit. One of the first strategic landmarks of Western culture was Odysseus's trick in the siege of Troy. The Achaean army left a giant wooden horse and pretended to leave for reinforcements. In reality, the army hid in a nearby bay, while warriors were concealed in the horse's hollowed belly.

From a different tradition, Sun Tzu advocated for deception as a key resource for warfare.

---

18 Green, 2008.
19 McKeown, 2015.

"When we can attack, we must seem unable. When using our forces, we must appear inactive. When we are near, we must make the enemy believe we are far away. When far away, we must make him believe we are near."[20]

On the same note, Robert Green stated that, in the game of power, "deception is the most potent weapon of your arsenal."[21]

The English language offers a rich vocabulary for describing prospective and future-oriented concepts. Words like goals, aims, objectives, purposes, intentions, and ambitions are frequently used. They are often interchangeable in our everyday conversations. However, these terms take on precise and distinct meanings in strategic planning.

For instance, "purpose" refers to the higher cause that a person or a company may have. It is the public good that the organization strives to deliver to society. Patagonia's "Save our Home Planet" exemplifies this. Or the purpose we devised for one of Latin America's top medical clinics: "Making better health possible."

In contrast to the purpose, an "objective" is a specific, measurable step in the path toward a larger goal. Long-term plans involve intermediate objectives, often referred to as "tactical." The problem is that "objective" often interchanges with "outcome." This is a dire mistake, as it blurs and erodes critical concepts of the SMM© model. That confusion not only strips off their crucial function but also hinders the correct wider sequencing of actions and tasks. To avoid this pitfall, "outcome" must define what you obtain when achieving the objective.

The distinction between these terms is of critical technical and methodological relevance. It's a baseline for clear communication and a

---

20 McCreadie, 2018.
21 Green, 2008.

condition for our messaging method. Thus, this book will categorize what people lousy refer to as "goal" into three specific terms:

> **Outcome**: the immediate goal of a specific communication act. It is what the audience does, as a result, in the same conversation, meeting, or presentation.

> **(End) Goal**: It is the final destination of my plan. Nothing comes after it. In the strategic streamline, it is located on the opposite side of the outcome, the starting point.

> **(Tactical) Objective**: Any step between the outcome and the end goal is an objective. Because of this middle ground, it is usually called a tactical objective.

Table 1 provides a brief definition and example of each, along with what they will be called in this book (See Table 1.)

TABLE 1

Type of goal	COMMUNICATIONAL	TACTICAL	STRATEGIC
Order	First	In between	Final
Definition	The aim of a particular communication act	A key measurable step to achieving your goal	The general goal you aim to achieve
Example	For the client to accept the terms of our proposal	Winning a big client's long-term contract	To increase permanent revenues
Referred as	Outcome	Objective	(End) Goal

The SMM© model focuses on actions that occur *ipso facto*, meaning at the exact moment when communication occurs. I am talking about concrete, particular interactions with the audience. They could be face-to-face conversations like a hallway chat with a colleague or a presentation to your boss. They could also be asynchronous interactions like an email to the IT department or a cover letter to a potential employer.

Those individual acts should also be part of a broader plan –a stream of actions that leads to achieving a mid-to-long-term strategic goal—so they have strategic value.

For example, you might have a long-term goal of becoming a manager, starting a business, or landing a new job. Once you define this goal, you can project a series of actions and envision how they will unfold. You can then develop a set of measurable objectives, which are steppingstones towards achieving your goal.

Let's illustrate this with some examples. Leading a high-profile project could position you well for a manager role. Therefore, getting your boss to choose you as the project leader becomes an objective aligned with your goal. Similarly, if you're starting a bakery, recruiting a master baker is crucial. In that regard, meeting with the best baker in town is a communication act whose intended outcome should be that the baker accepts my job offer.

This outcome is a crucial step towards achieving your ultimate (end) goal. Nevertheless, the same action that is someone's outcome can be someone else's objective (or even someone's goal.) This depends on each person's position within the strategic chain.

Take, for instance, the sales team of a German beermaking equipment company. This is a business-to-business (B2B) environment where the company has specialized teams for each product line. The team has one expert salesperson, Cornelius, a product manager named Isander, and a sales manager, Jafan.

The client journey within the sales funnel can be mapped through three key communication touchpoints. They are communication acts.

The first is typically a cold email introducing the company and its offering. This is followed by a meeting. Sometimes, it requires more than one session to delve deeper into the specifics. Finally, the journey culminates in a positive response from the client. That confirmation is usually via phone call or email.

In this case, Jafan, the manager, attended an international seminar on the future of beermaking. There, he met Zoraida, the supply manager of a local Mexican drought company. Excited about this potential lead, Jafan initiates contact by sending Zoraida an email proposing a meeting. Once Zoraida agrees, Cornelius, the expert salesperson, and Isander, the product manager, will take charge. They would attend the meeting to make Zoraida interested to the extent she asks for a formal proposal.

This is the expected outcome of the meeting for both Cornelius and Isander. Let us say they did it: Zoraida asked them to send her a formal proposal.

Nevertheless, in the next touchpoint, things differ. Cornelius' primary income comes from his commission for every closed deal. So, after sending the formal proposal to Zoraida (by email), Cornelius' (end) goal is for Zoraida to accept the proposal. This acceptance, typically a formal reply or email confirmation, marks the achievement of Cornelius' outcome. Through Zoraida's action, he secured a commission for a closed deal. Then, Cornelius moves to capture another client —and commission.

For Isander, closing the deal is not the ultimate goal but a crucial steppingstone – a tactical objective. His primary objective is to contribute to achieving the sales quota for his product line. This objective is formally validated during a video call meeting with the Board, where Isander presents the results.

Jafan, the sales manager, operates on an even broader scale. His ultimate goal lies at the end of each quarter when he meets with the CEO to review the overall performance of his area. Jafan's success is measured by securing the CEO's approval for the annual bonus for his entire team, based on the presented results and his explanation (see Table 2.)

TABLE 2

Touch-points		PHONE CALL	MEETING	EMAIL	VIDEO CALL	MEETING
Sequence		1	2	3	4	5
Audience		Zoraida		The Board		The CEO
Expected Action		To accept a first meeting	To ask for a proposal	To accept the proposal	To validate we met the goal	To approve the bonus
Sales Team	Cornelius	--	Outcome	Goal	--	--
	Isander	--	Outcome	Objective	Goal	--
	Jafan	Outcome	Objective 1	Objective 2	Objective 3	Goal

Understanding human emotions and moods is vital to strategically capitalizing on context. It involves understanding people and what inhibits or motivates them to act. Suppose people are part of our strategy (after all, in most endeavors, people are a driving force). When this is the case, it's essential to consider what might influence their behavior. If possible, consider the emotions that may cause or stop actions.

Let's take a real-life example. Imagine I'm addressing my colleagues after receiving a year-end performance bonus. It's safe to assume a generally positive mood in the audience. However, what if this bonus coincided with a company-wide layoff?

This scenario is not hypothetical. I once advised the VP of a large airline on his presentation for the annual general meeting. The company had just achieved promising financial results after two years of struggle. This was undoubtedly positive news.

However, there was another side to the story. That same year, the company had laid off 11,000 of its 55,000 employees (20% of its workforce). These layoffs were part of a cost-cutting plan proposed by a major consulting firm (yes, one of the Big Three.)

The annual meeting presented a complex emotional landscape. Employees and executives alike were likely dealing with financial difficulties. Fear, disappointment, anxiety, and anger were some of the emotions beneath the surface.

Diving into the good news would have been a grave mistake in this context. Likewise, a joyful or neutral presentation would have created a disconnect. It would have made the leadership seem insensitive to the plight of their own people.

So, how did the VP navigate this emotional minefield?

The first step was crucial. He had to acknowledge and validate their feelings by directly addressing the hardships faced by the audience. He had to show respect for those who were made redundant -the colleagues who became the "fallen" casualties of austerity and were no longer with us. This would show empathy, which was required in an almost ritualistic way. It was a necessary moment of shared grief. The audience can only be receptive to positive news after acknowledging this shared experience.

Sometimes, the audience's emotions are shaped by more than just the context. It can be rooted in pre-existing beliefs or values that may clash with the topic, the speaker or both.

For instance, a radical Muslim leader might not be open to a presentation on same-sex marriage. Similarly, an advocate for Intelligent Design might be skeptical of an evolutionary biologist. This extends to the topic of human evolutionary origins, even if the speaker is religious.

The more ingrained these emotional dispositions are, the less contingent they become; it is less about the context and more about the topics or the speaker's credibility or ethos.

We gain a big advantage when we grasp how the audience's emotions and context interact. Aristotle called this *pathos*. More than emotion per se, it refers to emotions raised by a speaker leveraging context. Demagogs and populists are experts on this.

Recognizing the relationship between context, audience, and goals and outcomes is vital to strategic mapping. First, they provide valuable inputs for leveraging context. From there, they can provide insights. These insights help tailor a message. It will resonate with the audience and aligns with our goals.

1.3. Recognize your Ethos

Another critical component for streamlining the strategy is the speakers' *ethos*.[22] The term comes from Aristotle's *Rhetoric* and refers to the speaker's credibility. Ethos is, in fact, one of the three sources of persuasive power, along with the audience's emotions (*pathos*) and the speech in itself (*logos*). "One is persuaded through ethos," said Aristotle, "when discourse is said in such a way as to make the speaker credible."[23]

Unlike trust or reputation, though, ethos is mainly rhetorical. This means it can be modified through discourse (*logos*), either decreased or increased. But to do so, you need to know your audience's perception of you.

First, you should acknowledge how much credibility you have among them and why. You can infer that by identifying the qualities or attitudes your audience values. Then, you refer to these aspects of yourself. We all do this explicitly when presenting credentials like degrees or work

---

22 In chapter 4.2, this concept is extensively reviewed in relation to its role within the model and its technical functionality with the discourse.
23 Bartlett, 2019.

experience. However, you can also do this more elegantly through a personal anecdote.

What qualifies as "valuable credentials" varies from audience to audience. For instance, a manager wants to gain the trust of their audience. In that case, their job title is significant because it speaks to their authority and position. Conversely, a scientist's credibility stems from their published research and grants. A war veteran's experience on the battlefield holds more weight than any job title or academic post.

Most of us have either succeeded or failed in communication challenges because of our ethos. Probably more times than we are aware of.

One of the times when the concept became most evident to me was when I tried to sell a training program to teachers. Not just any teachers but public-school teachers. My audience included the union leader, board members, and two teachers themselves. Although hired by a university linguistics department, I was introduced to them as a consultant. I sensed my credibility was low, so I tried to raise it by presenting credentials related to them. Then I said I was happy to be there because "I was a teacher, too."

"Where do you teach?" One of the teachers asked loudly, not making eye contact.

Hesitating, I backtracked, "No, I meant..." then mentioned I was lecturing at a university. My nervousness betrayed my voice .

The union leader delivered the final blow: "That's very different from being a schoolteacher."

The meeting ended swiftly, and needless to say, the sale fell through.

The problem here was that I didn't thoroughly recognize my ethos. My credibility was weak because I wasn't a public-school teacher. Being a young consultant from the private sector further diminished it. Even having a Ph.D. in Education from an Ivy League university wouldn't have helped. In fact, it might have backfired.

The key was building rapport by finding common ground. Not any, but one that helps me to be considered "one of them." I needed the "street credibility" of a schoolteacher. Yet that's only achievable by firsthand experience in a public-school classroom. They put in the hard work, the daily grind that forges a bond. Someone on the outside wouldn't truly understand.

Instead of claiming to be a teacher, I should have started differently. Perhaps by acknowledging, "While I haven't been a schoolteacher myself," I could have mentioned my mother's 20-year schoolteacher career, my experience in public schools, or how a teacher inspired my career path. Any truthful anecdote that showed recognition for their profession would have been better. Perhaps it wouldn't foster a stronger ethos, but it definitely would set a better ground from which to build credibility.

It can also be the other way around. The same principle applies to influencing ethos. Imagine a young professional presenting a project to a board of old-fashioned executives. Highlighting business experience might seem logical, but it could easily backfire. Focusing on upcoming digital trends or their digital native perspective would be much better. This is an area where this group of senior executives is mostly alien. However, they do know that it is important. In any case, you must always identify what would be your best source of credibility.

Your personal and professional background is packed with potential credibility sources. However, you need to understand which elements hold value for your audience. As these can vary significantly, recognizing your ethos is not straightforward. Yet essential. It's more impactful than you might think.

Understanding the context and your audience is crucial in this regard, as they determine the strength of your ethos. Ultimately, it all comes down to choosing the proper credentials to connect with your target audience.

1.4. Know your Audience

The audience is another crucial element for crafting a strategy, along with context, outcome, and ethos. Like presentation expert Nancy Duarte notes, most communication specialists stress capital importance.

Duarte recommends starting this process before you even begin preparing your speech. Ask yourself key questions about your audience's needs and how to address said needs. How can the information you provide improve the audience's lives? And what do you want them to do after the presentation?[24]

She even recommends creating a detailed audience profile. This implies evaluating their fears, opportunities, challenges, and current mood or state of mind. In that way, you can better understand the potential benefits of your message.

Of course, the more we know the audience, the better. But, while a comprehensive understanding of the audience is ideal, in practice this is not the case. Through working on messaging models, we've found that not every detail holds equal weight. Some are anecdotal or already included in a more comprehensive concept. Not all information will be equally relevant to your specific communication outcomes. This is because not all of it would serve the purpose of your strategy.

In that sense, Duarte's final recommended question is one of the most important: What specific action do you want your audience to take? In our SMM© model, we defined this as the outcome.

These four strategic variables –context, ethos, outcome, and audience—are are interconnected. They mutually influence each other. Therefore, a firm grasp of the context allows you to better identify and understand your audience. This, in turn, helps you define a realistic and

---

24 Duarte, 2008.

achievable outcome. Similarly, the better you know your audience and the context, the better you assess your ethos. A strong ethos allows you to set –and achieve– more ambitious outcomes. Conversely, a weaker ethos may require a more conservative outcome (see Table 3 and Figures 3 and 4.)

TABLE 3

	STRATEGIC COGNITIVE PROCESS							RESULT
VARIABLES	Knowing the context	⇔	Recognizing the audience	⇔	Assessment of my ethos	⇔	Setting the outcome	Reinforcing Loop (R)
RELATION	+	=	+	=	+	=	+	(+) Mutual reinforcement
	–	=	–	=	–	=	–	

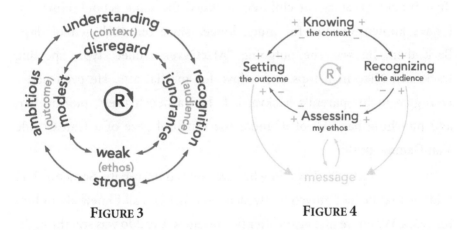

FIGURE 3   FIGURE 4

The previous table and figures (particularly Figure 2) used system dynamics (SD) notation. Its diagrams are great for illustrating how interconnected these strategic variables are.[25]

---

25 Forrester, 2017; Sterman, 2000.

However, the relationship between audience and outcome is even more profound. Together, they perform a key functional role as "semantic hinges." They are the joints that allow the transition between the strategic and linguistic realms. It is through them that strategic insights can become meaningful words.

The next chapter will explore how those hinges turn strategy into effective communication.

Before we move on, however, let's consolidate our understanding with a practical example. The story of Keops, a French Bulldog, will give you a comprehensive picture of how to outline a strategy. This example will demonstrate how this approach can be helpful not only in the workplace but also for challenges in your personal life and even at home.

This is also the story of Lucinda and Vivaldo. My wife and I became their friends because our children attended the same school. However, I have known Vivaldo for much longer since our high school days. Back then, he was the outgoing "MacGyver mullet" type, sporting tracksuits, Nike high-tops and a love for martial arts. He even had a DIY gym in his parent's backyard. It had a bench press, pull-up bar, and punching bag. All of it under the watchful gaze of a Jean-Claude Van Damme poster.

I lost contact with Vivaldo when we entered university. Someone had told me that he had moved to Sweden, and that was all I knew about him for years. When we met again after two decades, Vivaldo was still the high-spirited, outgoing guy I remembered. But his looks were very different. His appearance had undergone a complete makeover. He was now a "hipster dad" with skinny jeans and Caterpillar boots. The most notorious change, though, was his hairstyle. The joyful expanding mullet that cascaded from the back of his neck was gone. All that hair had moved forward to form a trendy, voluminous, self-contained quiff.

When I went to his home for the first time, I discovered his transformation wasn't just superficial. As I entered the door, he introduced me to Keops, a French Bulldog he called his "other son." Initially, the dog belonged to Vivaldo's sister. Still, after a bad mountain biking accident, she needed help with Keops while she recovered. Although she eventually got better, Vivaldo convinced her to let him keep the dog.

His sister agreed. However, his wife, Lucinda, refused.

After weeks of negotiations, Lucinda gave in to a compromise. Keops could stay on three conditions. The dog must quit three nasty habits. First, he had to stop rubbing himself on the pillows. Second, no more begging for food. Third and most importantly, Keops must stop sexually assaulting Silvio, a colorful unicorn that was their daughter's favorite toy. Vivaldo readily agreed.

But things stayed the same. Vivaldo kept watching his soccer matches and the UFC fights with Keops cuddled in his pillow. This meant that on the few occasions when Lucinda could nap, the first thing she'd see upon opening her eyes would be Keops' bare behind as the dog would be resting beside her head on the pillow. Vivaldo tried to keep his promise to Silvio the Unicorn by placing him on a high shelf, out of the dog's reach. But Keops interpreted this as the unicorn was playing hard to get. So, whenever Silvio wasn't on a high shelf, the dog went mental on him.

Lucinda tried to convince Vivaldo to return Keops to his sister, who also loved the dog. But Vivaldo always refused. The problem escalated, and soon, the subject became untouchable. I realized that in his quest to remove his deep-rooted 1980s "dudeness," Vivaldo went too far in his progressist transformation.

Every time Lucinda raised the issue, Vivaldo was dismissive. He criticized her for her lack of sympathy for animals. Whenever they argued, she would grow more exasperated and lose credibility with Vivaldo. Until she finally exhausted her ethos.

Imagine my surprise at their next dinner party –Keops was gone, and there were no signs of marital discord.

"How did you do it?" I later asked Lucinda.

"Strategy," she said.

The story was as follows. Lucinda took their daughter to the dermatologist during what seemed to be a persistent chickenpox case. It turned out to be allergic dermatitis, and the treatment included "avoiding contact with cats and dogs." Lucinda was in ecstasy. Now, she had everything she needed: a specific diagnosis, treatment for her daughter, and an ace up her sleeve for the Keops issue.

Yet, Lucinda remained cool. Instead of letting herself get carried away by this triumphant moment, she reflected upon it. She could have told Vivaldo, "I told you so," making him feel miserable and kicking the dog out. But she thought about her goal. This wasn't to teach Vivaldo a lesson or to point out how ridiculous his dog-loving millennialism could be. It was to get Keops out of the house. With this clear vision, she planned every conversation with Vivaldo to achieve that.

She did not lie or use deception. Vivaldo knew her dislike for the dog. It was already a touchy subject in their history as a couple and a family. Thus, Lucinda knew she had to tread lightly. She meticulously planned how to break the news.

What did she do?

First, she listed the doctor's guidelines. Medicine names, dosages, and instructions. A number of changes around the house followed, including removing goose down pillows and vacuuming the closets. At the end of the list, she wrote the final instructions for avoiding contact with dogs. This list and the doctor's prescription were sent to Vivaldo via WhatsApp.

Vivaldo acknowledged the message but didn't respond. When Lucinda returned home later that day, Vivaldo proposed cutting Keops' hair. He also suggested full deworming, disinfection, and grooming.

"Let's see how that works," he proposed as his last stand before considering sending him back to his sister. Lucinda simply agreed, "Sure, let's try it."

Because of her ethos, she had to act carefully. Lucinda's success hinged on maintaining credibility. A smug or triumphant phone call would have triggered Vivaldo's defensiveness.

Similarly, any pushback on his proposals or overplaying the doctor's instructions could have recoiled. These subtle mistakes can be fatal, often fueled by miscalculation or arrogance.

Lucinda kept a cool head. She remained composed, knowing the rash would likely return with Keops back in the house. Patience was key. All she had to do was play dumb on the subject.

One day before Keops' return from the pet groomer, Lucinda prepared for her final conversation with Vivaldo. Her outcome was to make him promise that if their daughter's rash returned, the dog would have to move out. However, things took an unexpected turn.

This time, Vivaldo approached her with the proposal. Seeing their daughter's rash-free face, he prioritized her well-being. He knew Keops was happy with his sister anyway, which made Lucinda happy, too. Keops' time with them had come to an end.

Lucinda's success was a fine example of applying strategic communication. First, she set a clear goal: getting Keops out. Then, she leveraged her understanding of the context (the rash and doctor's orders) and her knowledge of Vivaldo. She also took special care not to lose credibility by avoiding confrontation.

Finally, she crafted a course of action using tactical conversations with specific outcomes in mind (as seen in Table 4.)

Throughout the process, she anticipated Vivaldo's reactions and strategically positioned herself. It wasn't about brute pressure but slow, deliberate surgically precise moves to achieve her desired outcome.

TABLE 4

Comm.	WHATSAPP	CONVERSATION	
Sequence	1	2	3
Audience & Outcomes	Vivaldo to realize Keops may be causing the rash	Vivaldo to promise Keops is out if the rash returns	Vivaldo to agree on taking the dog back to his sister
Streamline	Outcome	Objective	Goal

KEY TAKEAWAYS OF CHAPTER 1

➢ Effective communication requires a well-defined strategy that considers the context, audience, objectives, and credibility.

➢ These variables are interconnected and influence each other dynamically.

➢ Strategic planning involves analyzing these variables to develop a roadmap for achieving communication outcomes.

➢ The SMM© model presented in this chapter provides a framework for understanding and leveraging these variables in strategic communication.

➤ Different types of goals (outcome, tactical, end goal) exist, and understanding their relationship is crucial for strategic planning.

➤ The audience emotions and beliefs significantly influence how they receive and respond to messages.

➤ The credibility (ethos) of the speaker is not just a tool, but a powerful lever that can significantly enhance the effectiveness of communication.

➤ Strategic communication is not limited to professional settings; it can also be applied in personal life situations to achieve desired results.

FIND THE HINGES

This chapter introduces the concept of "semantic hinges" as a bridge between strategic planning and crafting effective messages. It emphasizes the importance of defining clear, observable, and audience-performed outcomes that align with the overall strategic goal. The chapter also discusses the significance of identifying the audience's key motivation, which should be relevant, tractable, and achievable to drive them towards the desired action.

One shortcoming of strategic communications is that it often falls short in crafting the actual message. Detailed plans outlining what to do, how, and when are abundant, but guidance on what to say is scarce. For this, there are usually only general guidelines that should be more systematic. The lack of precise rules for linguistic content is a significant limitation, not only because of the critical role of clear messaging in today's communication but also because it misses out on the technical potential of language.

Introducing a novel approach to bridge this gap, we present two semantic hinges. As the name suggests, these hinges act as a joint between strategy and language. They facilitate the transition by converting strategic fundamentals into linguistic elements. Thus, they form the very foundations of the message itself. This novel solution was designed as a message-building tool. One that could be used by communication professionals, language experts and non-specialists alike.

The first semantic hinge is the outcome's target action, which focuses on the desired outcome, specifically the action the audience should take. The second hinge is the audience's key motivation, its action's trigger or driving force. Both hinges are extracted from a thoroughly analyzed and defined strategic plan.

The semantic hinges are not just abstract concepts but practical tools. They encompass a structured methodology, which must be tailored to its technical specs. Correctly applying these elements is crucial, as their integration is the key to success-specific wording. If you fail to integrate them, all is lost.

STEPS:

1. Think first, then plan.
2. **Find the hinges: target action and key motivation.**
3. Do the magic: build the message through an equation.
4. Bring that support: calibrate evidence and ethos.
5. Making it real: prepare the execution.

2.1. Hinge 1: Define the outcome as a target action

Another of the most common pitfalls in communication is failing to define a clear outcome. We often confuse goals, intentions, tasks and objectives with the actual desired result. Sometimes, this confusion gets tangled with performance metrics.

For instance, an insurance salesperson might aspire to a promotion. However, achieving that promotion hinges on meeting their sales target, which represents a tactical goal. Usually, they have key performance indicators (KPIs) like sales volume or conversion rate. To meet these metrics, the salesperson needs to close deals with clients. These deals typically happen during communication acts like meetings or, less likely, phone calls.

Here's the critical distinction: the desired outcome should be an action taken by the audience, not the sender. It should also occur during the communication itself, not later. In the sales meeting example, the desired outcome wouldn't be "to give a presentation." Here, the sender performs the action. However, if the outcome is for the potential client to "sign the contract," the audience performs the action.

This concept might seem counterintuitive. When asked about communication goals, many would say things like "deliver a presentation" or "provide feedback." However, these actions lie on the sender, not the receiver. As such, they describe a process, not an outcome. Effective communication aims to elicit results and mobilize people to act. It helps us in the challenge of getting things done through others, which is a leadership must.

A well-defined communication outcome hinges on three crucial conditions. First, it must trigger the audience to take immediate action. This action, on the audience's part needs to happen ipso facto, not ex-post. This means during the communication itself, not later on.

Let's illustrate this with an example. Imagine I'm having a performance review with Marsilio, a team member with anger issues. When stressed, he becomes verbally abusive towards colleagues. In this scenario, aiming for "learning to handle stress" as the outcome is wrong. While Marsilio might learn something, acquiring that skill takes time beyond our meeting. He cannot fulfil the action defined as the outcome (learning to handle stress) during our review.

Similarly, aiming to "stop mistreating others" wouldn't work either. This outcome represents a long-term goal requiring repeated actions over time. It might take months to determine if Marsilio has indeed addressed this issue. We will only know if Marsilio has stopped mistreating his co-workers after a long time.

So, what outcome would work? We need something achievable within the confines of the communication act itself.

Figure 5

Here's a better option: "for Marsilio to acknowledge his anger problem." The audience performs this outcome's action. Therefore, during the meeting, my central message must aim to get him to recognize his problem.

However, we can also induce these actions in the audience during the meeting. For example, "to understand that this is an ultimatum" or "to fear that I may fire him." Both actions are (i) performed by the audience and (ii) occur during the same communication act. So far, so good.

The third key element of a well-defined communication outcome is observability. Actions like "understanding an ultimatum" or "fearing being fired" are the audience's. But they happen internally and cannot be objectively verified. They're either cognitive (mental) or emotional. (See Figure 5.)

However, actions like "recognizing the problem" or "committing to specific deadlines" are observable. Both actions are also meant to be taken by the audience during the performance meeting. To categorize actions effectively, we must understand how they're expressed and consider the context.

Let's say you're meeting a potential client for the first time. It's unrealistic to expect them to hire your company right away. However, achievable outcomes for that first meeting could be for them to "understand your service." While this action involves thought (cognitive), it's not directly observable.

Author Nick Wreden highlights the importance of setting clear objectives from the start. This applies to anyone crafting an elevator pitch, for example. His advice: convince your audience to take the next step. This might be accepting a meeting proposal or requesting additional information. So, a more realistic outcome for the first client meeting would be "to get them to agree to a follow-up meeting" or "to get them to request a proposal."[26]

Knowing how to categorize target actions strengthens the persuasion process. I discovered its effectiveness when I succumbed to the sales ninjitsu of an old lady. This imposes a triple demand on their messaging. Leaders should be able to cast and communicate a clear, relevant, and truthful message. This is a challenging task, at least not without training.

---

26 Wreden, 2002.

That's why messaging is increasingly recognized as valuable. Its benefits add value not only for the individual but also for the organization.

But before going into the next practical example, let's return to the SMM© model for a moment. I built it using resources from different fields in a two-tier integration. First, it is a pragmatic consolidation of various disciplines. The principal areas are linguistics, strategy, rhetoric, and philosophy of language.

Second, I improved that consolidation with practical tools and techniques. I learned them all not from theory but from practice while working in different communication industries. This ranged from ad copywriter to marketing executive. From journalist to political speechwriter to communications and strategy consultant.

The model is a combination of different patterns that are integrated and coded into a single functional and self-contained unit.

Today, most of our work comes from repeat clients and word-of-mouth recommendations. This is mainly because of the ease and speed with which our clients can adopt the SMM© model. In a very short time, they grasped its value and applicability. Managers and executives from engineering or scientific backgrounds especially value the model, as it speaks to their technical nature, helping them articulate clear and compelling messages without depending or relying so much on talent or improvisation skills.

All examples and cases in the book are genuine. These situations actually occur. I have changed the names and details of people and events, especially the sensitive ones. Yet, I put special care into ensuring each situation depicts what happened.

Back to the case in point. One winter afternoon, I received a call from a gentle, trembling-voiced woman who sounded like my grandmother. "Hello?!" I'm Cordelia, but everyone knows me as Cookie."

I wasn't far off in my guess. She told me that, aaages ago, she had been my mother-in-law's schoolteacher.

My mother-in-law had given her my number because I was such a "fine, generous young man."

After a few more pleasantries, she asked: "Would it be possible to visit you this Friday afternoon? I want to show you a financial product that turns your tax returns into an investment."

I said no. I was too busy. Cookie insisted. I held my ground politely. We said goodbye, and that was it (I thought.)

Two weeks later, I was checking my emails at home when my wife approached me. She gently touched my shoulder and said,

"Darling, why don't we buy the insurance Cookie told you about?"

I looked at her, surprised.

"Listen, it's a good product," she added. "It wouldn't cost us much, and she's such a sweet, poor old lady."

As it turned out, Cookie had spoken to my mother-in-law, who, she knew, would talk to my wife. Cookie did not cheat or trick me. She leveraged her knowledge of relationships, motivations, and sympathies to her sales advantage.

More than unethical or deceitful, she was a strategic saleswoman looking to close a deal. She outsmarted me. And so, I, the so-called communications expert, had to call Cookie to ask her to come over.

She came. I signed. Just before leaving, she handed me a notebook and a pencil. I looked at her. And she said, "Please, darling, write for me the names and phone numbers of five of your closest friends."

She was a real sales ninja.

Cookie had her communication objectives down. The cold call's aim wasn't to make the sale, as one might expect. Her outcome was for me to accept the meeting proposal.

When I refused, she immediately pivoted and asked to visit another time. Both actions –accepting the meeting or setting a date– meet the three criteria. They are observable, audience-performed, and immediate.

Faced with my initial resistance, Cookie identified an alternative path. My mother-in-law. The outcome would be for my mother-in-law to agree to talk to her daughter (my wife) about the insurance.

Finally, once face-to-face, Cookie's communication outcome was for me to sign the contract, which I did.

Categorizing target actions is a valuable skill beyond the professional realm. These principles apply universally in business, politics, social interactions, and family situations. They're crucial whenever you aim to persuade or motivate someone. The table below provides a framework for applying this categorization of actions. Each is presented in context as part of a real-life communication challenge.

They clarify and define a specific communication outcome (see Table 5.)

TABLE 5

TARGET ACTION	CONDITIONS		
Setting A: investor's roundtable	It is carried out by the audience	It occurs on the spot	It can be observed *
1. Pitch my start-up to a group of investors	X	✓	✓
2. For one of the investors to invest in my start-up	✓	X	X
3. For an investor to decide to invest in my start-up	✓	✓	X
4. For an investor to give me his card saying, "Call me"	✓	✓	✓

Setting B: meeting with my team	It is carried out by the audience	It occurs on the spot	It can be observed *
5. To improve my team's performance (KPIs))	X	X	X
6. For my team to improve its performance	✓	X	X
7. **For my team to commit to improving its performance**	✓	✓	✓
Setting C: presentation to a potential client	It is carried out by the audience	It occurs on the spot	It can be observed *
8. For the potential client to hire a consultancy	✓	X	X
9. For the potential client to recognize our added value	✓	✓	X
10. **To schedule a follow-up meeting**	✓	✓	✓
12. **For the potential client to request a proposal**	✓	✓	✓

Only five of the dozen actions from Table 5 qualify as well-defined communication outcomes: actions 4, 5, 8, 11, and 12. Let's apply this framework with a personal example. Imagine I'm harboring a dream of living in Frutillar, a lakeside town in Chile's Patagonia. Founded by German settlers in the 19th century, it's a popular summer destination. Yet lately, it has also become a growing hotspot for young, middle-class families. However, I know my wife might not share my enthusiasm. While she agrees Frutillar is perfect for summer vacations, she might see it as too cold, rainy, and isolated for year-round living. Knowing this, I need to strategize my communication approach. The most suitable tactic is casually introducing the idea during a relaxed conversation. Now, let's set a realistic target action: "for my wife to consider the idea of moving to Frutillar." My wife would take this action, and it would also happen during the conversation itself. Therefore, it fulfils the first two criteria for a well-defined outcome.

Here's the interesting part: even though "considering" is a mental process, it can be observed through her verbal response. A positive response like "maybe" or "let me think about it" would be different from a dismissive "Are you nuts?" or "Not again… (see Table 6.)

TABLE 6

TARGET ACTION	CONDITIONS		
Setting: proposal to my wife that we relocate	It is carried out by the audience	It occurs on the spot	It can be observed *
1. To convince my wife to move to Frutillar	X	X	X
2. For my wife to move to Frutillar	✓	X	✓
3. For my wife to say she will consider the idea	✓	✓	✓

Here, only action 3 fulfils all three criteria for effective communication outcomes. A well-designed outcome serves two essential purposes. First, it clarifies our understanding of the other variables at play in the situation. This newfound clarity becomes crucial when we need to reframe our message for better impact.

Furthermore, a well-designed outcome leads to a clear and concise expression of it. It translates into a simple sentence with a specific structure. This structure consistently sets together three key pieces of meaning: the audience, the action, and the result.

The audience becomes the subject of the sentence. The verb represents the action, which aligns with the communication outcome we defined. Finally, the object of that action becomes the grammatical complement (see Table 7).

TABLE 7:

STRUCTURING	AUDIENCE (subject)	+	ACTION (verb)	+	OBJECT (compliment)
	[For] My boss		to approve		the action plan
	My team		to commit		to improving performance
OUTCOMES	My partner		to accept		foregoing a bonus
	The Board		to approve		the proposal
	My wife		to agree		to consider a move

The strict grammatical organization we use for communication outcomes is crucial. It allows us to translate strategic variables into clear, actionable words. These words are the building blocks of our message. They will also form the essential components that make up the SMM© equation.

2.2. Hinge 2: Leverage your audience's key motivation

Defining the outcome is one of the tasks for finding the hinges that would allow the transition from strategy to linguistics. The other task is to find the audience's key motivation.

First, motivations have two natures. One side is driven by interests, which are typically objective. These are what learning psychologist Beth Hennessey calls extrinsic motivations. They focus on achieving an external goal or meeting a need imposed by something outside of us.

Interests are also often linked to a person's role or position. Employees, for example, are naturally interested in their salaries. A general manager, on the other hand, is most interested in the company's profitability. Because they're concrete concerns, interests are often expressed in measurable terms. They are usually the same or equal to key performance indicators (KPIs).

Let's take a local mayor as an example. Defining the mayor's key motivation as simply "power" is too broad. The same goes for "the well-being of their constituents." While options like "re-election" or even "popularity" are more specific, they can still admit further refinement.

Ultimately, a mayor's strongest motivation is likely "votes." The mayor wants to be popular, but in a way that directly translates into securing votes. Votes are a politician's most valued asset and the ultimate measure of success. Media presence, donors, and money all contribute to popularity. That popularity is sought after and has value to the extent that it translates into votes. And not any but votes within their constituency. This is the ultimate, most concrete and valued interest of a mayor.

For a government minister, things are different. Popularity is still paramount to their job, but not because of votes. For a minister, popularity is measured by other metrics. Their primary concerns are public recognition and approval ratings for their specific ministry. These are the indicators that matter most.

Here's a real-life example I encountered while working as a speechwriter for Chile's Minister of the Interior. One day, the Minister of Transportation, a reserved academic type, arrived at the office. After introductions, the Minister of the Interior (his boss) went straight to the point. "Listen," he said. "I don't care if people know you for being good or bad, as long as they start knowing you! Do something about that before our next meeting."

So, just like a mayor, a government minister needs popularity. However, how they achieve that popularity differs. Votes reflect a mayor's popularity, while approval ratings measure that of a government minister. Both require popularity, but the tangible expression of that popularity is distinct. This distinction can lead to seemingly contradictory situations.

Let us exemplify this with a case. It is portrayed in Kàs, a popular tourist spot on the Turkish Riviera. Yet, it could happen in any Mediterranean tourist hotspot. Turkey's Ministry of Environment, Urbanization and Climate Change released its latest report, revealing that pleasure boat trips must be cut by half to save marine wildlife on the coastline. According to national polls, 90% of the Turkish people support the measure. They are adamant about preserving their environmental, cultural, and historical heritage. In contrast, the local population, which depends heavily on tourism, opposes the initiative.

Supporting this initiative would gain public recognition and approval ratings for the minister and the mayor of Kàs. However, this only benefits the minister in the long run. In the immediate term, the mayor is most concerned with votes - the votes of the 30,000 adults in Kas County. He sees the nearly 65 million national voters as irrelevant, along with national television viewers and the world at large. Unless the mayor aspires to a national political role, only local voters matter.

Motivations can also be mapped to personal needs and the longings or pain points of individuals or groups. These motivations can be extrinsic, driven by meeting an externally imposed factor. However, they can also be intrinsic, based on the desire to do something for its own sake or the enjoyment of the task itself.

Suppose you're a newly promoted 32-year-old credit risk manager at a bank. You're new to the role and the company and must prove yourself to your boss and colleagues. There's another, more experienced credit risk manager at the bank, who doesn't need the same validation you do. Their focus is on avoiding mistakes that could tarnish their reputation or jeopardize their retirement. As risk managers, the junior and senior colleagues both share the common interest of limiting risk. This is an essential part of the job and KPIs. But personal motivations differ significantly.

The message-building formula of this book relies on understanding the audience's motivations. So, we must identify the motivation that most compels the audience towards the outcome. This chosen motivation must align perfectly with the target action we want them to take. Otherwise, we risk sending a message that triggers a different, unexpected action. Even worse, it can ignite an action that directly contradicts our intention.

For any motivation to be a persuasive tool, it must meet three critical criteria. First, it needs to be highly relevant to the audience. In simpler terms, it has to matter to them. Second, it must have traction. This means it should be closely linked to the specific action we want the audience to take. Finally, the chosen motivation must be achievable. Once incorporated into the message, it should feel realistic and believable. It should represent a promise you can keep, an offer you can deliver on, or a situation that is likely to happen.

The more evidence you can gather to support the chosen motivation, the easier it becomes to integrate it into your message. Take, for example, using "quality of life" to convince your spouse to move to Frutillar. Evidence for this motivation might be readily available. Just use population density, crime rates, and traffic congestion data. However, finding evidence is much more challenging if you choose "professional opportunities." The seasonal nature of a small summer town always limits the number of permanent jobs.

2.2.1. Relevant to my audience, not to me

While working as a speechwriter, I learned a valuable lesson about the dangers of making assumptions. It happened during an official visit to Paso Los Libertadores border control. Built in the middle of the Andes Mountains, the facility is 3,000 meters above sea level and is the connecting passage between Chile and Argentina.

By that point, I'd been with the minister for a while. I was familiar with the competitive, luminary-centric nature of frontline politics. Everyone with political aspirations jockeyed for a position at the minister's side. This became incredibly pushy when the TV cameras were rolling. The closer you got to him, the more attention you received. The brighter the core, the more concentrated the political gravitational forces. This was the place where elbow nudging, ass-kissing, and back-stabbing were on full sway.

Staying too far on the periphery, however, could also be risky. It could be interpreted as a lack of commitment or closeness to the minister. And, before you know it, you are excluded. An intermediate distance was a much better option, at least for me.

However, each orbital ring required different tricks. For the inner, most sycophantic circle, it was crucial always to look concerned and in the know. They acted as if they were always onto something of the highest importance. In contrast, people who orbited in the second ring, like me, needed to look busy. We had to seem as if we were working on something utterly important.

We were travelling by official government helicopter, a quick 30-minute journey from Congress. The trip also involved a significant altitude change from sea level to 3,000 meters. To make matters worse, I was battling a hangover from a night of partying that ended at 4 A.M. Needless to say, altitude sickness hit me hard. Because of that, I was caught off guard.

Disoriented by the headache and separated from the minister's group, I ended up in a computer room with a senior officer from Chile's civil police. With great enthusiasm, he insisted on showing me a new border control software program they were developing. This software would link data between Chile and Argentina, streamlining the border crossing. That would eliminate the need for travelers to go through passport control twice.

Four months later, we launched the software with much fanfare. It received widespread media coverage across newspapers, radio, and television. The minister himself delivered an inspiring speech on continental unity and collaboration.

However, at the office the next day, I was met with strained greetings from an anxious secretary. She quickly pulled me aside. The software had malfunctioned, and the minister was furious. "Bring me the idiots in charge of this charade," he had demanded. That meant the senior border control officer and me. We sat outside the minister's office, waiting to be called in. I cast a complicit, sympathetic glance at my colleague. After all, we had become friends over the past four months. He was highly anxious: I could see sweat beading on his forehead, and the dark, wet spotting on his armpits and belly. While nervous myself, I tried to project a sense of calm. "Listen," I reassured him, "the worst that can happen is we get fired."

Instead of calming him down, he looked at me with terror in his eyes. It was the worst thing I could have said. Instead of comforting him, my message did the exact opposite. The road to hell is paved with good intentions.

This is a common but strategically disastrous mistake with catastrophic consequences. It is a product of projection —— the tendency to see things from our own perspective and apply our experiences to others. In this case, I projected myself onto the senior officer, a man in his 50s with vastly different circumstances. I assumed his interests, needs, age, values, and career goals mirrored mine. I projected my entire self onto him.

See, my friend's reality was utterly different from mine. Retirement was on the horizon for him, and a demotion would directly impact his pension. Additionally, this was his first and only job, one he had entered in his early 20s. His closest friends, perhaps even his wife, were likely part of the civil police force. This wasn't just about his job but his entire life. My complete misread of the situation caused my message to have the opposite effect. It exacerbated an already stressful situation. I had made a bad situation worse.

A similar incident occurred in October 2019 involving Chile's Transportation Minister. During an interview about a metro fare increase, he made a seemingly harmless remark that may have cost him his career.

"If people want to pay less," he suggested, "they can wake up earlier." Perhaps naively, he meant that people could avoid the fare increase by taking advantage of the lower fares offered at dawn. This unplanned comment, now infamous, enraged the Chilean public. It became the trigger for a social explosion of protests that lasted for months. The outrage stemmed from the context of the remark. It looked too likely that that minister has never taken the metro himself.

Stress, haste, and intense emotions can all lead us to project our own experiences onto others. We speak before we think, creating a common but potentially explosive situation.

I remember another occasion early in my consulting career. I was working at a Spanish bank when I bumped into Taltibius, a university friend in the sales division. When he learned I worked in communications, he eagerly asked me to review a presentation he'd been working on with his team. It showcased a new credit card offering airline miles for purchases – a novel concept at the time.

"This is a no-brainer," he said. "It's a winner. All our projections show it will sell like hotcakes. It targets a lucrative segment – middle-class clients. I've even presented it twice to the credit risk manager, who needs to sign off on it. But he keeps saying he'll 'give it another look' and sends us away. Why can't he see the potential?"

What happened to Taltibius has probably happened to many of us. We often get excited about ideas that align with our own interests. In Taltibius' case, his focus was naturally on boosting sales. However, this enthusiasm can blind us to the fact that our audience might have different priorities. This, in turn, can lead to a negative response, the opposite of what we intended.

For Taltibius, sales were the holy grail. Monthly KPIs, like sales growth and profit margins, measured his performance. However, a higher sales volume for the credit risk manager also meant a higher risk profile.

Taltibius and I took a moment to reflect on this. We realized the target customer base was young professionals and middle-class earners. This segment generally corresponded to a low-risk profile.

Later that day, Taltibius tweaked his presentation. He shifted the focus slightly, highlighting the low-risk aspect of his proposal. This resonated with the credit risk manager, who gave the green light the next day. The key takeaway? Taking a moment to pause, reflect, and consider what the credit risk manager truly cared about made all the difference. It was about empathy and understanding his priorities.

2.2.2. Traction towards my outcome

Last year, I witnessed a powerful example of how choosing the right motivation can make all the difference. Our team worked with Cassandra, the union leader of a struggling hydrocarbon company. She needed to craft a critical speech for the upcoming union general assembly. The company and the country as a whole were facing a severe economic downturn that was expected to worsen. The union members became increasingly agitated, pushing for a strike to secure a bonus.

Cassandra, however, was aware of the risk of layoffs if management felt pressured by the strike. So, she struck a deal with the CEO: the workers would forego the strike, and the company wouldn't lay anyone off for the next six months.

Cassandra used the SMM© model. She defined the outcome of her speech in the union assembly as getting the union to drop the idea of striking. This fits the criteria —an action (no strike) taken by the audience (workers), observable through a vote during the assembly.

Cassandra knew that most workers were genuinely interested in receiving their year-end bonus. So, she was initially tempted to focus on the bonus, a clear motivator for the workers. However, she realized that the bonus motivation clashed with her goal. Given the company's financial state, they would never receive a bonus this year, which presented a roadblock.

The solution came from a shift in perspective. Cassandra recognized that everyone was aware of the looming economic crisis. She leveraged a more long-term motivation: to have a job in difficult times. By widening her vision, she took a new approach to the workers' motivations. That new perspective helped Cassandra to surpass a strategic gridlock.

This experience highlighted the importance of context. Every client in every industry responds to unique circumstances. Some are specific to their sector, others to the situation. It is crucial to pay close attention to the context, its nuances, stakeholders, and their motivations.

The two cases above illustrate the critical role of strategic analysis. Without identifying the right audience motivation, there is no possibility of traction. This is why it's always better to consider multiple potential motivators. Because that gives me more options to choose from. In the case of the union workers, two motivations emerged: (a) avoiding job loss and (b) minimizing the need for a difficult job search during a recession.

This broader understanding increases the chances of finding a "motivational sweet spot." A motivation that makes the audience do what I want them to do. Knowing the individual within the audience can further refine this strategy. For example, HR managers share the same interests in the standard KPIs of their role. These include productivity, talent acquisition and retention, and employee engagement. They also juggle concerns about absenteeism, accident rates, and union relations.

For instance, two HR managers, Pampinea and Polonius, share these interests and assess their work by them. However, while Polonius has five years of experience in the role, Pampinea was just appointed. Also, she is perceived as "too young" by her boss. Therefore, Pampinea would need to prove her boss wrong alongside the shared KPIs. Polonius is fifty years old and has just been the father of new twins. His new life circumstances call for flexible work arrangements and remote work options. This variety of motivations within the same role requires a versatile approach. One that could work in a structured and tailored way simultaneously.

One of the first times I implemented this approach was when I helped Ismene, the export manager of a prestigious new world winery. She needed to prepare for a meeting with Malcolm, a British distributor, to raise the price of their best-selling wine.

After careful reflection, Ismene established the outcome's target action. She needed Malcolm "to accept the price increase." This action fulfilled the critical criteria. It was an observable action performed by the audience (the distributor accepts.) It is also meant to occur within the communication act (the meeting.) Now, when we looked at the motivation, someone highlighted that what Malcolm was most interested in was that we didn't raise the price of wine.

Ismene recognized that this conflicted with our objective. The question then becomes: How can we reconcile this? First, it is key to recognize when a motivation undermines or opposes our goal so we may dismiss it. Then, we should look for a motivation that aligns with the outcome. If not, the desired outcome itself might need to be adjusted.

However, a well-developed strategic analysis often reveals alternative motivations that fit our goals.

Like Cassandra's situation, we untied the knot by taking a broader view. We shifted the focus from a specific audience's motivation to a more general, strategic one. We recognized that price is a tool to achieve sales, which in turn generates profits. Therefore, the distributor's fundamental interest wasn't simply avoiding a price increase. Ultimately, it all came down to protecting their earnings (see Table 8.)

TABLE 8

OUTCOME	MOTIVATION TO LEVERAGE	RESULT
For the British distributor to accept the price increase	For the price not to be raised	=> <= contradiction
	Maintain their profit	=> => traction
To convince the workers not to go on strike	To receive the bonus	=> <= contradiction
	To maintain their jobs	=> => traction

In short, an audience's motivation should meet three conditions to be persuasive. First, it must be relevant to the audience. Second, I need to have traction aligned with my outcome.

FIGURE 6

Third, it should seem possible to achieve or comply with when added to the message (see Figure 6.) The link between messaging, chance, and proof is vital. We will go deeper into this later in this book.

2.3. Setting the building blocks

Envision the action that you want your audience to do and their principal motivation. When these elements merge, they form the bedrock of a potent message. This integration doesn't just invigorate your communication. It brings new perspectives, focus shifts, or even new narratives. It helps you shape the conversation by establishing a message's new 'semantic territory'.

In Cassandra's case, the original scenario was a simple one-way cause-and-effect. The strike led to the bonus. However, by introducing the concept of "job security," the conversation shifted. The bonus became a secondary element, overshadowed by a more relevant and urgent one. The concern of keeping their jobs. This transforms the relationship between the elements into a two-way causality (see Figure 7.)

TABLE 9

SEMANTIC HINGES	
Outcome's Target Action	**Audience's Key Motivation**
For the workers to give up the strike	To maintain their jobs next year

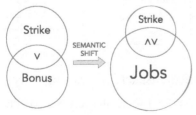

Figure 7

Figure 8

The choice of verb in your message is pivotal. It's not just a word. It's a connector of two distinct ideas, the driver of their relationship of crafting impactful messages. Verbs define the fundamental meaning of a sentence. They are also significant and instrumental in creating new meaning.

As we previously saw, a compelling verbal message should comply with three conditions. First, it must carry a clear judgment. Second, it must be expressed with straightforward syntax and a single, unambiguous meaning. This judgment can either be pushed in the direction of benefits or potential harm. (See Figure 9 and Table 10.)

FIGURE 9:

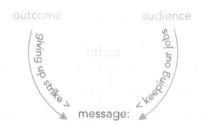

Giving up the strike **assures** we keep our jobs next year

TABLE 10:

MESSAGE			SENSE
Target Action	**VERB**	**Key Motivation**	
Giving up the	will protect	Our jobs for the	Obtaining a benefit
Strike		next year	
Going on	will put at risk		Avoiding harm

So far, we've delved into the linguistic aspects of crafting effective messages. Now, let's shift gears and consider the strategic point of view. This perspective empowers us to understand how the message equation works. The message should be constructed as a correct response to the following question: How can I leverage the audience's motivation (building block 1) to push them towards my outcome (building block 2)?

Remember, the right building blocks are crucial. Despite the approach, creating effective messages can still be intuitive. In fact, I've witnessed people successfully crafting impactful messages on their first attempt. This highlights the value of your role in the process and the potential you have to make a significant impact.

KEY TAKEAWAYS OF CHAPTER 2

> Effective communication requires a well-defined strategy that considers the context, audience, objectives, and credibility.

> Semantic hinges are crucial tools for converting strategic fundamentals into linguistic elements in communication.

> A well-defined outcome is an action performed by the audience during the communication itself, which can be observed.

> The audience's key motivation must be relevant, have traction towards the outcome, and be achievable.

> The message SMM© equation involves leveraging the audience's motivation to push them towards the desired outcome.

> Verbs play a crucial role in connecting ideas and driving the relationship between the outcome and the motivation.

STEP 3

DO THE MAGIC

This chapter focuses on building strategic messages using the SMM© equation. It provides instructions on how to apply the equation, along with practical examples of the formula in real-life challenges. The text then delves into the distinction between judgments and assertions, examining their different communicational roles and showing how and why strategic messages should always be well-founded judgments. It also shows that, when thoroughly applied, the SMM© equation has the virtue of producing concise messages that address the audience's motivation with clear syntax and a single, unambiguous meaning. Additionally, the chapter guides on using the equation when addressing multiple motivations within both singular and multiple audiences, providing the how-to for crafting effective messages in such situations.

Marshall McLuhan's renowned quote, "the medium is the message," encapsulates an insight. The medium is not a passive conduit.[27] Instead, its very nature and form actively shape the message, thereby influencing its significance. "The medium does something to people," he observed. "It takes hold of them. It rubs them, massages them, and hits them."

---

27 McLuhan, 1996.

The influence of form in communication extends beyond the medium. The speech act that conveys it is equally significant. It's not the same whether the message is couched in an assertion, question, order, threat or promise.

In his seminal work, *How to do Things with Words*, philosopher John Austin coined the term 'performative utterances' to describe these choices. He recognized that these utterances are not mere descriptions of the world. They have the power to transform the world around us by reshaping social reality.[28]

A classic example is the saying "I promise" between the bride and groom in their wedding ceremony. This isn't just a statement. It's a speech act that actively produces a new reality.

Let's say you are in love with the bride. It is different to declare your love to her before or after her marriage vow. You have many more chances of running away with her if you declare your love before, as Hollywood has shown.

This variability presents a double challenge for the message's semantic integrity. First, the specific context or use may affect its meaning. It can shift depending on the situation.

Second, the whirlwind of multidirectional flows makes contemporary communications ubiquitous, multi-media, and multifaceted. This implies high exposure to polysemy, which opens the door to misunderstandings and dispersion.

All this brings a growing significant challenge within organizations. It hampers the achievement and maintenance of the much sought-after organizational alignment.

This is where the significance of effective messaging in leadership becomes most clear and needed. Leaders must possess the ability to

---

28 Austin, 1975.

persuade, mobilize, and unite others towards a shared goal. Clear and unambiguous messaging is crucial in aligning these diverse interests.

It is also key for giving meaning to daily tasks and instill a sense of purpose in individuals and teams.

Of course, all messaging must consider situational, pragmatic variables. They are, indeed, part of the context as a strategic condition. However, while the "how" of communication matters, the most valuable aspect of a messaging technique lies in the "what." Its main contribution must be guiding on what to say on a *propositional* level, at its semantic core.

Strategic messages must be clear and unambiguous, as they induce or align action. However, they must also resist the variability caused by the situation and the medium. Therefore, they must be performative utterances with sound semantic stability.[29]

Besides clarity, strategic messages must be relevant. This means they need to communicate something that truly matters to the audience.

As brand expert Nick Wreden advises, "If people do not hear what is in it for them, they will not listen to you."[30] By focusing on the "what," leaders can ensure their messages resonate with the audience and prompt the intended action.

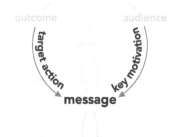

STEPS:

1. Think first, then plan.

2. Find the hinges: target action and key motivation.

3. **Do the magic: build the message through an equation.**

4. Bring that support: calibrate evidence and ethos.

5. Making it real: prepare the execution.

---

29 Davidson, 1984.
30 Wreden, 2022.

3.1. Build the message using an equation

Having explored the building blocks of effective messaging, let's delve into the core formula itself. This formula, at its heart, is an equation to guide your communication. It asks the essential question: What do I tell an audience X, whose motivation is Y, to make them do Z?

Think of X, Y, and Z as variables to be plugged in. "X" represents the specific audience you're targeting. "Y" captures their key motivation, the underlying reason for making them receptive to your message. Finally, "Z" defines your desired outcome –the action you want the audience to take (further explained in Table 11, which we'll discuss later.)

This formula provides a clear framework for crafting targeted and impactful messages.

By understanding your audience (X), their motivations (Y), and your desired outcome (Z), you can tailor your message to resonate and drive action.

TABLE 11:

SMM© MESSAGING' EQUATION		
Elements	**Question**	**Formula**
X = Audience Y = Audience's Key Motivation Z = Comms. Outcome - Audience's Target Action	What do I tell an audience X, whose motivation is Y, to make them do Z?	$= f\,(X, Y, Z)$

As shown in Table 11, the SMM© equation can be expressed as a question or function. The question makes it easy to apply the formula.

Everyone can follow this approach by simply replacing the variables in the equation ("X," "Y," and "Z") with the strategic key elements (see Table 12.)

TABLE 12

SMM©MESSAGING' EQUATION	
Example 1	**Example 2**
What do I tell **the workers (X)**, who are interested in **keeping their jobs (Y)**, to give **up** the idea of **going on strike? (Z)**	What do I tell the **British wine distributor (X)**, whose motivation is **maintaining their profit (Y)**, to **accept** the **price increase? (Z)**

Then, you generate the message as the *answer* to the SMM© equation's question. So, the message is also the equation's *result* (see Table 13).

TABLE 13

EQUATION > QUESTION				RESULT > MESSAGE		
What do I tell [audience X]	...who want/s to [motivation Y]	...to make them do [outcome Z]	=	Communicate the outcome's target action	Verb	Audience's key motivation
British distributor	maintain profits	accept the price.		The price increase	will not affect	your profit
The workers	keep their jobs	dismiss the strike.		Dismissing the strike	would ensure	we keep our jobs
The minister of energy	being popular with young people	accepting to criticize the dam	=	Publicly criticizing the dam project	will make you	popular with young people
My beloved wife	enjoy a better quality of life	consider moving to Frutillar		Living in Frutillar	would mean	a much better quality of life
The Credit Risk Manager	lowering and controlling risk	approve the new credit card		The new credit card	entails	very low and easily controlled risk
My climbing partners	reach the summit and	agree on starting walking at 2 am		Starting to walk at 2 am	will help	us reaching the summit

The SMM© equation includes another linguistic pattern. This makes building the message even more structured and technical. We did not aim to identify a specific tactical outcome. Instead, we aimed for a more general strategic one.

On the left side of the equation is the outcome's *target action*. That semantic hinge must be defined and organized, as seen in Table 2. This is audience *plus* action *plus* object (see Table 2). The hinge on the right side of the equation corresponds to the audience's *key motivation*.

FIGURE 10:

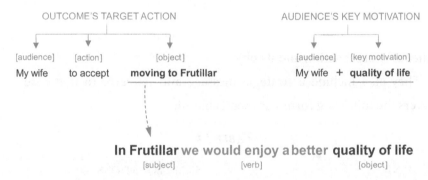

Then, the outcome's object and the audience's key motivation form the sentence together. The message is made by combining the outcome's target with the audience's key motivation. A conjugated verb performs that combination (see Figure 11.)

There are two critical steps here. First, we turn the target of the outcome's action into the message's subject. Second, we turn the audience's key motivation into the object of the new sentence. Therefore, the message must be a sentence. Its subject is the target object.

Similarly, the sentence's compliment should be the audience's primary motivation. We saw this before. The formula of the messaging provides the framework for the narrative. Now, the SMM© equation allows us to go technically further.

It indicates the exact words and their place in the sentence (see Figure 12).

FIGURE 11:

Suppose we assign values to the parts of Outcome "Z." These are the audience's target action and its object.

They also include a strategic message and its verb. In that case, it delivers the following formulas (See Table 14.)

TABLE 14

ELEMENTS	SMM© EQUATIONS		
X = Audience	Communications	Strategic Message	
Y = Aud. Key Motivation	Desired	Standard Notation	Cobb-Douglas
Z = Outcome's Target Action	Outcome		Function
A = Aud. target action	$Z = X(A + O)$	$M = A(O) + V + X(Y)$	$K_X(\frac{1}{Z})^{\alpha}(Y)^{\beta}$
O = Target action's object			

Table 14 shows different notations of the SMM© equation. It can also be expressed as a Cobb-Douglas production function.

Because it obeys a structured method, the equation forms a technique.

It is something that anyone can learn and apply. With some practice, this messaging *technique* can quickly become a messaging *skill*.

Moreover, the technique's strength lies in its strategic foundation −it's built for real-world use.

This also translates into its significant versatility; the SMM© equation can be applied across diverse situations and formats.

In fact, it has consistently delivered clear and relevant messages throughout the cases presented in this book (see Table 15.)

TABLE 15

STRATEGIC MESSAGES	WORDS
The price increase will not affect your profits.	8
Criticizing the project will make you popular with young people.	11
Dismissing the strike will ensure keeping our jobs next year.	10
STRATEGIC MESSAGES	WORDS
In Frutillar we would have a better quality of life.	10
Starting to walk at 2 am increases our chances of reaching the summit.	12
The new credit card entails very low and easily controlled risk.	11

Finally, Table 15 showcases the power of this messaging technique in action. All the resulting messages are concise, practical, and efficient. They capitalize on audience motivation while staying remarkably brief – typically within 7 to 12 words. This

Keynote speakers' mentor Tricia Brouk provided a specific word number as efficiency rule. She said we should keep our ideas within 15 words. "Even if it is a good idea," she warns, "you have to be able to communicate it in 15 words or less."[31]

The messages resulting from our SMM© model align perfectly with Brouk's efficiency rule. Consistently, the SMM© equation technique helped us achieve messages that are 25% to 50% leaner, exceeding Brouk's recommendation.

---

31 Brouk, 2018.

3.2. Use judgments' sensemaking power

Among all speech acts, judgments and assertions play a crucial role in our grasp of the world. They are not only the most used in understanding our experiences but also in referring to and making sense of them. While judgments and assertions serve distinct purposes, they often work together in a complementary way.

Assertions deal with objective, verifiable truths – commonly called "facts." Logicians refer to their "truth value," meaning they can be definitively proven true or false. Their primary function is to establish veracity in spoken communication.

Judgments, on the other hand, express interpretations and explanations. They inherently involve a viewpoint, never presenting facts in isolation. This makes them statements of opinion or evaluation, often reflecting the speaker's stance or intention. Judgments essentially offer a "verdict" on reality.

As you delve deeper, you'll realize that judgments and assertions are not in conflict. On the contrary, they work hand-in-hand. Assertions provide the factual foundation. Judgments, with their perspective, help us apply those facts in specific situations. Their complementary nature is one of the key distinctions of effective communication.

Assertions tend to be longer sentences that require more effort to process and understand them. They also sound nerdy or even dull. That is why we prefer judgments much more. They are more accessible and practical. In fact, in everyday life, most people rarely back their opinions with facts, and listeners are usually okay with this. But there is a limit.

If your views are on a subject where there is a disagreement or your opinions are too strong, you need robust data to support them. Otherwise, you could be seen as opinionated or judgmental, and that's not good.

Because both opinionated and judgmental people tend to jump to their semi-preconceived conclusions, therefore they are seen as less analytical and more biased. This undermines their person's credibility and, thus, their speech: both ethos and logos.

For example, "In high-altitude mountaineering, those making the summit attack should return to camp by noon." This is a judgment expressing a viewpoint based on certain facts. It's not inherently true or false on its own.

In contrast, "More than 90% of avalanches occur between 12 am and 4 pm" is an assertion. It's a verifiable statement that can be proven true or false. Similarly, "Three-quarters of mountaineering accidents occur on the descent" is another assertion.

Judgments become crucial in interpreting the meaning of asserted facts. For instance, a judgment might follow the assertion about avalanches. "By returning before noon, we avoid exposure to avalanches." This connects the asserted fact to its practical implication. Another judgment could be. "We also must give ourselves extra time for the descent, which is always dangerous." (See Table 16.)

Now, imagine yourself climbing Illimani, a 6,438-meter peak in Bolivia's Cordillera Real mountain range. A sub-range of the Andes, each day it receives the moisture from the Amazon lowlands. The rapid ascent turns this moisture into blizzards and snowstorms, which can rage on for three hours, usually between 11 am and 2 pm. This weather pattern explains Cordillera Real's glaciers so close to the equator.

The judgment "In the Cordillera Real, expect midday snowstorms for a few hours" is critical. It can even be potentially life-saving information (See Table 16.) This example highlights another crucial function of judgments. They transform past experiences into valuable guidelines for the present and future. Climbers who have experienced midday snowstorms in the past now know this. We navigate uncertainty by forming judgments from past events to inform our decisions.

TABLE 16

JUDGMENTS	ASSERTIONS
1. In high-altitude mountaineering, those making the summit attack should consider returning to camp at noon. 2. By returning at noon, we avoid exposure to avalanches. 3. We must give ourselves extra time for the descent, which is always dangerous. 4. In the Cordillera Real, it always snows at noon for a few hours.	(i). More than 90% of avalanches occur between 12 am and 4 pm. (ii). Three-quarters of mountaineering accidents occur during descent. (iii). There is an 80% probability of snow in the Cordillera Real tomorrow at noon.

Regardless of the available evidence, a strategic message should always be a judgment, never an assertion. The supporting evidence, however, should be firmly rooted in assertions. Knowing when to present a judgment and when to rely on assertions is an essential linguistic (pragmatic) competence.

Presentation expert Nancy Duarte emphasizes this point: "Slides that show data are not really about the data," she argues. "They are about the meaning of the data." She adds, "Most presenters miss this distinction. How many times have you endured a presentation where the speaker drones on about a complex chart, leaving you clueless about the key takeaway?"

Thinkers throughout history have not just recognized but celebrated the power of judgments. For Aristotle, rhetoric aimed to shape judgments, not deliver assertions. Judgments bridge the gap between meaning, emotions, and perception. He says emotions make men fickle and change their judgments because "pleasure and regret arise from them."

This tendency is particularly pronounced in mass audiences. The ancient Greeks called them the *hoi polloi* or the "multitude." Their modern equivalents might be "the people" or "the masses." Aristotle sustained that this audience responds primarily to achieve pleasure and avoid pain. Judgments, therefore, can induce, modify, or suppress emotions. They take advantage of emotions' ability to steer the discourse towards either getting a benefit or avoiding harm.

Along with this psychological role, judgments act as vectors of shared meaning. Research in organizational psychology has also been studying collective action. Their findings have shown how people act according to the narratives they are immersed in. Such narratives provide frameworks that ascribe meaning to their collective experiences. This process is often referred to as "sensemaking." Judgments, in this context, offer new reference points to link ideas and actions. Not just among these same ideas and actions but also with broader networks of meaning. In this sense, they can modify the frontiers of our world.

For all these reasons, judgments are natural conduits for meaningful, impactful messages. They are ideal vessels for carrying either honey or poison, full of strategic intent. As Seth Godin puts it, "Communication is about getting others to adopt your point of view." It's about "helping them understand why you are excited (or sad, or optimistic, or whatever else you are feeling.) If all you want to do is share facts and figures, cancel the meeting and send a report instead."

Let's explore how this plays out in practice with a comparison of two press clippings (see Table 17). These differ in scope, audience, and style. The first belongs to the *Daily Mail*, a British daily tabloid. The other text is from a research paper published in the peer-reviewed journal *Ecological Economics*.

The Daily Mail's audience has been described as insular, middle-aged British nationals. Most of them with conservative views. The *Journal of Ecological Economics*, in contrast, addresses the scientific community. As such, it is internationally minded by essence.

TABLE 17

SOURCE	JUDGMENT	SUPPORTING ASSERTION
The Daily Mail[32]	[These three High Court Judges are] enemies of the people. [There was] Fury over "out of touch" judges who defied 17.4 million Brexit voters and could trigger a constitutional crisis.	MPs last night tore into three 'out of touch' judges for ruling that embittered. Remainers in Parliament should be allowed to frustrate the verdict of the British public.
Journal of Ecological Economics[33]	Two features […] seem to appear across societies that have collapsed: the stretching of resources due to strain placed on the ecological carrying capacity, and the division of society into Elites (rich) and Commoners (poor). [Either feature] can independently result in a complete [societal] collapse.	Since the regrowth of Nature is optimum when $y = \lambda \,/\, 2$, we can find the optimal level of depletion (production) per capita, δ^* in an egalitarian society where $x_E \equiv 0$, $\delta_{**}(\geq\delta_*)$ in an equitable society where $\kappa \equiv 1$, and δ^{***} in an unequal society where $x_E \geq 0$ and $\kappa \, N \, 1$.

The first example is a controversial Daily Mail headline. "Enemies of the People" cried the front page on November 4, 2016, in the wake of Brexit. Here, the headline pushes forward a judgment, turning an interpretation into a powerful label: ["These High Court Judges are] enemies of the people." This label served as the core message of the article and, by extension, the entire newspaper.

It was also the key message of the entire newspaper. In most influential tabloids, a front-page headline is a communication act in itself. This is a crucial reason why tabloids are so influential. They put messages on the streets that reach millions of people daily. Their words appear in front of people's eyes, including those who don't buy the newspaper.

The second example, a research paper in ecological economics, presents mostly scientific information. Although it may surprise some, the

---

32 The Daily Mail, 2016.
33 Motesharrei, 2014.

key message of the piece is also a judgment. Of course, this judgment is firmly supported by sound, evidence-based assertions. These assertions contain facts and quantifiable data from empirical testing and modeling. Still, the research paper's conclusion and key message are judgments.

Judgments often receive bad press because of their lousy use. People frequently use them in many sleazy, foolish and even dirty ways. But don't be fooled by this. Judgments are a serious business. Their potential for manipulation and spin is their greatest peril, so experts approach them suspiciously. Yet, they are invaluable communication tools. Judgments excel not only in conveying persuasive messages that are strategic and action oriented. They are also fantastic tools for providing explanations, summarizing ideas and encapsulating insights.

Most research papers and technical reports communicate their "conclusions" using judgments. Of course, these findings must have been thoroughly supported. They are the result of analysis, testing, and modeling. But they are—and must be—judgments anyway.

A risk manager's story illustrates this point. He was very frustrated with how his new junior analysts presented their cases. They showed facts and figures without reaching a clear judgment. "If they keep presenting me facts, they aren't doing their job," he said.

The meetings were supposed to last ten minutes at most. They were just meant for validation and decision-making, the last part of a process. "I needed to know if that company or business is a yes or a no and why. Sound and quick. Instead, they start telling me this and that, showing me Table X and Graph Z." He then concluded, "I don't need reporters. They are analysts, for Christ's sake!" A script template solved the problem. It required all cases to conclude with a judgment followed by a recommendation.

Let's now look at another real-life example. The outdoor gear company Patagonia is campaigning against an energy project in the central region of Chile, near the capital Santiago. A hydroelectric plant would draw water from a river to supply energy for a mega-mining project.

The problem is that, to do so, the plant must intervene in the basin of a river that is the source of water for a city of more than 5 million inhabitants. This, plus the irregularities in its approval and the current scenario of climate change and water scarcity, mobilized several environmental and citizen organizations to oppose the project.

Patagonia's activism team wants to bring the country's minister of energy on board. Let's say the plan is to convince him to publicly criticize the project. While this is ambitious, it is worth a try.

To this end, Patagonia's team defined the desired outcome "to get the minister to agree to publicly criticize the project." They knew the minister needed to raise his profile and popularity. The easiest way to do so was to gain the favor of young adults. This was a demographic segment that strongly opposed the dam. It was also one of the most sympathetic to the government.

Therefore, the strategic message could highlight the potential benefits for the minister. For instance, "Publicly criticizing the project will make you popular with young people." Conversely, it could address the potential harm. "Not publicly criticizing the project will make you unpopular with young people."

Supporting evidence for the first statement (benefit) could be found effortlessly. The last national poll by Gallup showed that 95% of young people between 15 and 40 oppose the project.

This is an assertion, a statement of fact. It provides veracity, not direction. As such, it can support either of the two judgments above, both positive and negative, benefit and harm.

On the other hand, a judgment is an interpretation or evaluation of the assertion. For example, 'Publicly criticizing the project will make you popular with young people' is a judgment. One that can be inferred from the assertion that young people oppose the project.

Similarly, in Chapter 2 (see Table 5,) union leader Cassandra needed the workers to abandon their planned strike. This was to pressure management for a bonus.

However, management planned to use the strike as an opportunity to reduce costs through layoffs.

Cassandra negotiated a deal with the CEO: no strike, no layoffs. Her message, a judgment, focused on both the benefits and harms of both options, providing a comprehensive picture for the workers.

The table below (see Table 18) summarizes how judgments and assertions were used in these two real-life cases. It showcases the possible strategic messages that could work in either situation despite their differing directions.

TABLE 18

SITUATION	(to obtain a benefit) ← SENSE OF THE MESSAGE → (to avoid a loss)	
1. Patagonia's activist meeting with the Minister of Energy	(a) Publicly criticizing the project will make you popular with young people.	(b) Not publicly criticizing the project will make you unpopular with young people
	(c) Ninety-five percent of young people (15-40 years) oppose the dam project, according to an in-depth survey published by Gallup International last week.	
2. Labor union leader's speech in the general worker's assembly	(d) Dismissing the strike will safeguard our jobs for at least another year.	(e) Going on strike will put our jobs at risk next year.
	(f) Despite the losses the company sustained this year and an additional 25% loss projected for the year ahead, the CEO promised me yesterday that if we don't go on strike, there won't be layoffs next year.	

This rule and pattern can be applied to most messages seen (See Table 19.)

TABLE 19

SETTING	OUTCOME'S TARGET ACTION+VERB+AUDIENCE'S KEY MOTIVATION		
Labor union leader's speech in general worker's assembly	Giving up the strike	will protect	our jobs next year.
	Going on strike	will put at risk	maintaining our jobs next year
Winery export manager's talk with a British wine distributor	The price increase	won't harm	your profits.
	Not raising the price	makes it difficult	to continue our business.
Patagonia's activist meeting with minister of energy	Publicly criticizing the dam	will make you	popular with young people.
	Avoiding criticizing the dam	will make you	unpopular with young people
Sales Manager presenting to credit risk manager	The new credit card	may end up	lowering our average risk exposure.
	Not having the credit card	may increase	our average risk exposure.
Talking to my wife about relocating	In Frutillar, we	would enjoy	a much better quality of life.
	Not moving to Frutillar	is missing	an opportunity for a better quality of life.
Planning the summit day with climbing partners	To start walking at 2 am	helps us	reach the summit and return safely.
	Start walking later than 2 am hampers our chances for summit and safe return.		

3.3. Clear syntax and one sense only

In his seminal book *Thinking Fast and Slow*, Nobel prize winner Daniel Kahneman shows how our brains have a dual processing system. That system drives our thinking and choices. One is intuitive, metaphorical, impressionistic, automatic, and (of course) fast. At the same time, the other is slow, deliberate, and requires attention and effort. Slow thinking always takes over when things become complicated. But, as it is lazy, it usually accepts what the "fast" says anyway.

This is why, according to Kahneman, clarity is the first and most important rule for a persuasive message. It must also be simple and concise. "The best thing you can do", he says, "is to optimize readability to reduce cognitive effort."[34] Simplicity helps the brain's "processing fluency," recognizes writing consultant Bill Birchard. So, short sentences, familiar words, and clean syntax are a must. They ensure that the reader doesn't have to expend much processing energy.[35]

From a linguistic perspective, a message is much clearer if the syntax is simple. This often involves using the active voice instead of the passive or reflective voice. Neuroscience and neuroimaging experts who conduct empirical research on language agree. Passive voice lowers comprehension by 10%. It uses more words than the active voice, making comprehension even slower (See Table 20.)

TABLE 20

SENTENCES	VOICE	Word Count
(a) A giant tsunami hit Japan.	Active	5
(b) Japan was hit by a giant tsunami.	Passive	7
(c) Young investors value social returns.	Active	5
(d) Social returns are valued by young investors.	Passive	7

---

34 Kahneman, 2011.
35 Birchard, 2021.

The same cognitive attrition applies to sentences with clauses. They take 1/10th of a second longer to understand than clause-free sentences. Moreover, clauses use commas, which also introduce a pause.

Suppose you combine passive voice with clauses; the effect multiplies. The sentence and message become even more challenging to read (see Table 21.)

TABLE 21

SENTENCES	Voice	Clauses	Words	Comas
(a) Social profitability, a metric that, unlike classic ROI, does not consider only monetary profit, but also calculates environmental and added social value, is valued by young investors.	Passive	3	26	5
(b) Young investors value social profitability. This metric calculates environmental and added social value instead of the classic ROI, which considers only monetary profit.	Active	0	23	0

Another practice that muddles a sentence's syntax is including conditionals or arguments. Both a conditional and an argument come to life as *relations*.

They are functions. Therefore, they always have at least two different elements. It is part of what constitutes them.

As the Table shows, conditioning can be performed in two main ways. You can use 'if' at the start or middle of the sentence or introduce conditionality into the verb (see Table 22.)

TABLE 22

SENTENCES	Words	Commas	Verbs
(a) "**If I wake up** too early, **I will be** a zombie for the whole day"	15	1	2
(b) "**I will be** a zombie for the whole day **if I wake up** too early"	15	0	2
(c) "Walking up too early **would make me** a zombie the whole day."	12	0	1

Usually, conditioning through the verb uses fewer words, comas, and verbs. This is indeed the case for option (c) of Table 22. The problem with options like

a) is that 'If' produces a sentence of two phrases separated by a comma. "If X, you get Y." Similarly, a sentence like

b) doesn't have a comma but involves two separate elements. The relationship -if- is also weak in merging the elements into new meanings. It puts them together. That is why, most of the time, conditioning like

c) is the best option for strategic messaging. We will examine this more closely in the next chapter.

On the other hand, when a sentence contai0ns an argument, it may include commas. Yet the sentence almost always ends up as a compound of two elements. Prepositions or connectors of causality explicitly express the relationship between them. "We do X to get Y." "By doing X, we got Y." The following Table (See Table 23) shows the differences in sentence structure. The six sentences communicate the same content but with different syntax and effects.

TABLE 23

SENTENCES	Words
(a) To ensure our business relationship, we must raise the price.	10
(b) We must raise the price to ensure our business relationship.	10
(c) A price raise is necessary to ensure our business relationship.	10
(d) If we raise the price, we ensure our business relationship.	10
(e) A price raise ensures our business relationship.	7
(f) Raising the price ensures our business relationship.	7

Of the six sentences in Table 23, options (e) and (f) use fewer words. They do not have commas, conditionals or arguments.

Sometimes, the problem is more semantic. Although expressed in the message's syntax, its root lies deeper. This is usually the case for messages with two or more competing meanings. That is a big issue, and it can mean a big mistake. Strategic messages must be univocal, which means having one unequivocal sense—one and only.

A key to detecting this problem is whether the sentence contains a comma, an "and," or two verbs. Any of these three things can mean danger. As we saw, commas are often used to insert clauses into sentences. However, commas may also be used to enumerate a list. The elements of this list may have equivalent or competing meanings. For instance, consider the following sentence. "The experience of having a child was unexpected, stressful, marvelous, and hard." The syntax is short and straightforward. Yet, its keywords (unexpected, stressful, marvelous and complicated) have different semantic directions.

This may be a valid and eloquent reality to express. Still, in terms of messaging, all these adjectives make unity of sense challenging.

Using "and" to join two nouns is usually safe but using "and" for verbs is dangerous, because you could be sending two messages by having more than one active verbs on both sides of the sentence. These two messages are syntactically presented as one but are displayed as two. In Table 24, sentence (A) contains two propositions, whereas sentence (B) contains only one.

TABLE 24

SENTENCE A	1	The NOAA **oversees** tsunami risk <u>and</u> **rules it out** for Japan.
PROPOSITIONS	2	(i) The NOAA oversees tsunami risk. (ii) The NOAA rules out tsunami risk for Japan.

SENTENCE B	1	The NOAA rules out tsunami risk for **Japan** <u>and</u> **Korea.**
PROPOSITIONS	1	The NOAA rules out tsunami risk for Japan and Korea.

Now, a strategic message is not any message. It is one whose primary virtue is its capacity to impact.

To influence or mobilize people in real situations. So, it is quintessentially an applied message, a message in context. This determines its syntax, semantics, and pragmatics.

3.4. Messaging more than one motivation

However, when you analyze the audience, you often find multiple motivations. A mayor should be interested in votes, of course. But also, in improving the quality of life in the community or making the most of his position to become rich. Human resource managers should care about productivity. They should also care about recruiting talent and improving the work environment. The audience may also be more than one person. This happens in boards or committees, where two or more people decide (and, thus, the target action.)

Suppose I oversee community relations for the company where I work. The company manufactures stainless steel industrial kitchens and their equipment. One of our factories is in a municipality home to the country's largest forge for years. So, I propose a trade school project with senior neighbors who were former forge workers. The project is with the municipality. Therefore, I had to convince three people to approve it. They are the mayor, the company's human resources manager, and the public affairs manager. As there is no time to meet with each individually, I must present to the three of them in one hearing.

The problem is that they have quite different interests. The mayor is interested in his constituents. The corporate affairs manager cares about the reputation and community liaison. The HR manager is interested primarily in productivity. He also cares about skill development and training. Considering our formula's principles, one may be tempted to address each person's top interest. Then, include the three of them in the message (See Table 25.)

TABLE 25

'SMM© EQUATION					
ELEMENTS	Audience	X1: the mayor X2: PA manager X3: HR manager	Motivation	Y1: votes Y2: reputation Y3: productivity	Outcome Z: give their ok to start the project
QUESTION	What do I tell an **audience** X, whose **motivation** is Y, to make them **do** Z?				
EQUATION	What do I tell **the mayor (X1), PA (X2), and HR (X3) managers,** who are interested in **votes (Y1), reputation (Y2), and productivity (Y3)** to **give their ok to start the project (Z)**				
MESSAGE	"The community trade school could bring us **votes, reputation** and **productivity**"				

In this case, the message would be as follows: "The community trade school could bring us votes, reputation, and productivity." The problem with this message is that it loses unity of sense.

The other direct alternative is to choose one of the audience's key motivations. Suppose we go for productivity. The message will be "The trade school could improve productivity."

Here, there is not only one problem but two. One is strategic: the message only alludes to the interest of a single decision-maker. This misses a chance to use the motivation of another critical person in the audience. It also fails to address his interests. This may produce bias.

The other problem is structural. Monopolizing the message makes one of the three equal interests stand out. It closes the chance for alignment and reduces speech coherence. It becomes impossible to form a proper, sound argument or topic sentence.

TABLE 26

STRUCTURE		Function	Speech Act
The community trade school can bring us productivity gains.		Key message (yes)	Judgment
↓	↓		
[because...] It would win votes for the major.	[and...] It could contribute to our company's reputation.	Arguments / Topic Sentences (no)	Judgments

"The community trade school project can bring us productivity gains *because* it would win votes for the mayor *and* could contribute to our company's reputation" doesn't make sense. So, in cases where we want to leverage more than one motivation (n+1), the formula should be applied with a crucial variant.

First, you apply the messaging equation to each key motivation of the audience that you have decided to leverage. Do this as if it were the key message—one by one. As shown in Table 27 (see Table 27) the messages are correct. They combine the two key parts of the outcome's target action and the audience's key motivation.

TABLE 27

EQUATION > QUESTION					RESULT > MESSAGE		
What do I tell [X]	…who want/s [Y]	…to make them do [outcome Z]	=	Comm. outcome's target action		Verb	Audience's key motivation
The mayor	Votes					win us	Votes
PA manager	Reputation	Give their ok	=	Approve the trade school project will/would		benefit	Our reputation
HR manager	Productivity					bring us	Productivity gains

The three resulting sentences are strategic messages. But none is made central. When leveraging more than one motivation, the main message is different. It is not here because it comes from the other side of the formula. It comes from one hinge and not from combining them. It comes from the action the outcome aims for. Thus, the central message is usually a straightforward verbalization of the target action. Or a by-product of it, with some elaboration but always generic enough to embrace the key messages (see Table 28 and Figure 13.)

TABLE 28

STRUCTURE			Function	Speech Act
You should give the green light to the trade school.			Central message	Judgment
↓	↓	↓	Key messages (+Arguments)	Judgments
[because…] It would win votes for the mayor.	It would benefit our reputation.	It can bring productivity gains		

FIGURE 13

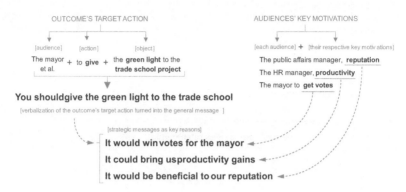

This messaging formula variant allows for more than one audience's motivation (n + 1). It expands the reach and usefulness of the SMM© model and equation. On the one hand, it lets you address groups of people with different interests. An example is the recent trade school project (see Figure 8.)

On the other hand, it allows the audience to be addressed individually. It uses not just one but two, three, four, or five motivations to persuade. This may be less effective in situations with limited time and attention spans, like advertising or marketing. However, it is handy for internal communications. I have seen it work perfectly in presentations, meetings, and talks, which are usually longer.

I choose whether to leverage one motivation (n) or more than one (n+1). I base that decision on the time and media available, the audience, and my outcome. Suppose the communication act is too significant, or the stakes are high.

In this case, I recommend thoroughly planning. First, developing and elaborating the two options. Then, I will compare them, both in script and performance. Finally, pick the best one and practice its execution several times.

Let's do this with one of the former examples presented in the book (see Figure 14 and Table 29).

FIGURE 14

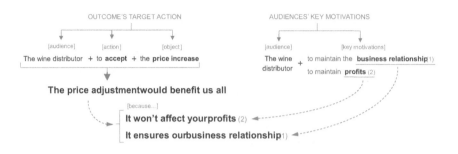

TABLE 29

One lever	Two levers
The price adjustment won't affect your profits. Six months ago, Vinovio Ltd. transferred the increase directly to 80% of its clients and its profits have not fallen.	The price adjustment would benefit us all. **It won't affect your profits**. Six months ago, Vinovio Ltd. transferred the increase directly to 80% of its clients and its **profits** have not fallen. It **ensures our business relationship**. We are operating at cost due to the rise in oil prices and new tariffs introduced last year.

As you may have noticed, this method of applying the strategic message is within a more elaborate construction. It is at the level of the speech, not the message.

However, despite its power, I have preferred to leave it out of this book. It goes beyond the message: a single key point that can be stated in a sentence. For now, the formula can be applied successfully.

When there are multiple motivations, the explicit speech must have at least three sentences: two key messages plus the central one. Each key message should address each audience's motivation. The central message, in contrast, should encompass them, either verbalizing the communication outcome or providing general meaning and direction.

KEY TAKEAWAYS OF CHAPTER 3

➢ Strategic messages should be judgments. They should express interpretations and evaluations based on factual assertions.

➢ Clarity and relevance are key. Messages should be simple, concise, and focused on the audience's interests.

➢ The SMM© equation is a formula for crafting effective messages. It brings together the desired outcome (the target action I intended to induce in the audience) and the audience's key motivation into a new sentence. It and it answers what should I say to an audience X who is interested in Y to make them do Z?

➢ The formula also works with multiple motivations, whether addressing an individual person or a group. When doing so, tailor the central message to encompass multiple motivations in the arguments, while maintaining clarity and coherence.

➢ Judgments and assertions work together. Assertions provide factual support for judgments, which provide meaning and direction.

BRING THAT SUPPORT

In this chapter, we review the relationship between truth and rhetoric in communication, highlighting the importance of credibility (ethos) and factual evidence. It also delves into the role of assertions in supporting well-founded judgments. The text also explores the impact of cultural context and shared knowledge on the effectiveness of communication, emphasizing the need to tailor messages to the audience's understanding and beliefs. Additionally, it examines the role of modal verbs in calibrating the intensity of messages based on the strength of evidence and the speaker's credibility.

ethos

message

evidence

STEPS:

1. Think first, then plan.

2. Find the hinges: target action and key motivation.

3. Do the magic: build the message through an equation.

4. **Bring that support: calibrate evidence and ethos.**

5. Making it real: prepare the execution.

n the previous chapter, we showed that the message must matter to the audience. To cast that relevance, we rely on judgments' sensemaking power. These are the most suitable speech acts for communicating and leveraging meaning. They can bring forth a new reality, which is why Nietzsche said a judgement's value lies in its power. These are the possibilities opened by the interpretation, explanation, or revelation they provide.

However, truthfulness is also essential. The audience must believe that the judgment being communicated is possible and likely to occur. It must also be delivered in good faith, without the intention to mislead or confuse. Failing to be truthful undermines the message and harms the speaker's credibility. This can cast doubt on later messages from the same source. So, it's vital to keep the process credible.

The risk of losing credibility can cause severe harm. It affects both personal and public communication. It can affect our daily messages with friends, family, and colleagues. However, it can also affect the messages of politicians, companies, and the media. Naturally, we tend to place less trust in those who only talk the talk than those who walk the talk. The same applies to political and advertising messages. Although they are usually mediated, "you must be able to believe it to buy it," warns Frank Luntz. "If your words lack sincerity and contradict facts, circumstances, or accepted perceptions, your message will not make an impact."[36]

To understand what comes next, we must go back to the roots of rhetoric. Ancient Greek philosophers and rhetoricians reflected on the power of language and its relationship with truth, meaning and action.

According to Aristotle, rhetoric is not an exact science. Like logic, science is about the necessary (*ananké*) of what is always true or false. The objects of rhetoric, in contrast, are always open to reasonable doubt. They do not have absolute certainty. In this world, situations can unfold in several different ways. They are also open to a range of interpretations.

---

36 Luntz, 2007.

That is precisely why we can make judgments. Because we can consider the possibility of their opposite. This is because, in all such matters, said Aristotle, plausibility guides judgment. It all comes down to what, under certain circumstances, a person will be inclined to believe is true. Because of this, there is room for technical manipulation (*téchne*).

Rhetorical plausibility is not like math. It responds to experience. In this realm, patterns and tendencies are never absolute. However, they can appear so if a tendency is consistently repeated (Taylor Swift writes her own songs.) This repetition embeds the tendency in the collective mind. It shapes public opinion, even if it's only partially true. In this way, a contingent reality can become a given or set one. For instance, consider the statements in Table 30:

TABLE 30

JUDGEMENT			PROBABILITY
Subject	Verb	Object	(a) Almost certain
1. Brazil	could eventually win	(i) a future World Cup	(b) Very likely (c) Likely (d) Possible
2. United States			(e) Unlikely
3. China		(ii) the next World Cup	(f) Very unlikely (g) Almost impossible

These statements show how judgments predicate empirical probability. For instance, "China's national soccer team could win the World Cup." That is a real but distant possibility. The possible event is so unlikely that few would consider giving it a second thought, let alone a wager. In contrast, "Brazil could (eventually/conceivably) win the World Cup" is very possible because it has done so in the past. Several times. This statement has predictive value. It's like a statistic's linear regression. It predicts according to the existing data.

Therefore, matching the judgment with the correct probability matters greatly. And for that, reference is vital. The judgment must precisely refer to semantic objects, categories, and extensions.

Of course, the more I know them, the better I know what to say. For instance, the probability that Brazil could win is almost 100% if our reference is all future World Cups. However, the odds change significantly if the object shifts to FIFA's next World Cup. It will be in North America in 2026. For Brazil, it goes from very likely to possible. As for Argentina, in this same case, the odds range from very likely to very unlikely. This is because Argentina just won the 2022 World Cup in Qatar. In the 22 World Cups, no champion has won twice in a row.

Perceived probability is not just from individual judgment. It is heavily influenced by culture and shared knowledge. I recall explaining the World Cup to an American friend unfamiliar with soccer. When she asked me about the best team, I replied.

Today, Argentina is the best team, but Brazil may be better. Germany always makes it through and almost always wins.

—What?

I realize how ludicrous this may have sounded. However, a big gap between our sports cultures made it sound even sillier. For Americans, sports should be big-time entertainment with many highlights and scores. If you miss one of them, the match offers many breaks so you can see them again on television.

Contemporary soccer is entertainment. But it is also the battleground of European Nationalism —a "war by other means," said George Orwell. This merged with Latin America's flair for dancing and soap operas.

I stuck to the facts via an assertion to give my friend a coherent explanation. "Of the 200 nations that have participated in the 22 World Cups, only nine have won," I explained. Brazil has won the most, five times, followed by Italy and Germany, four times each. Then comes Argentina with three wins, France and Uruguay with two, and Spain and England with one win each." From there, she could draw her conclusion.

The less shared culture, the less shared knowledge. And the less shared understanding, the more assertions are needed. "Cultural differences are a nuisance at best and often a disaster," said intercultural expert Geert Hofstede. The less context is shared, the easier it is to slip into misunderstandings and pitfalls.

Usually, an opinion can be expressed without backup. But strategic messages should be different. Shared experience allows a judgment to be considered valid before any evidence. It is substantiated and credible. This is only possible if the assertion is in our shared view. Understanding becomes more elusive and less confident when the audience is diverse.

In any case, as they are never true or false, judgments should rest on assertions to be truthful. That's why strategic messages should always be well-founded judgments. They should always include a supporting assertion and refer to the evidence, with their verbs calibrated accordingly. Therefore, judgments must always be elaborated and worded regarding supporting evidence. Even if the evidence is never explicitly addressed or mentioned in the speech.

Once we share a familiar world with our audience, there are two sources for making a credible judgment. One is the speaker's credibility; the other is the weight and availability of evidence. These sources are also correlated. The more credible I am for the audience, the less supporting evidence I need. Inversely, the less credible I am, the more evidence I need to gather and show.

4.1. Making facts useful again

A few years ago, I was flipping through TV when I stumbled upon a popular show. It was called In Your Own Trap and was inspired by the BBC show The Real Hustle. A team of journalists orchestrated elaborate stings. They did this in each episode to expose scams by turning the tables on con artists. This time, the target was a street game called "Where's the Froggy."

The game was a cunning hoax. The hustler was a seasoned operator known as "The Veteran." He would shuffle three cards in front of the victim. One featured a fancy frog in a top hat, while the others remained blank. The game was simple: guess the card with the froggy and win the pot. Miss, and the house takes all.

The interview was in the Veteran's cell. The Veteran has been behind bars several times for this scheme.

"What do you plan to do once you leave?" asked the journalist.

"Back to work, of course," replied the Veteran, smiling. "This world is so full of fools. Every time I'm back on the streets, there are more... You pick up a rock, and a dozen suckers crawl out."

Then, he added, "With the right words, you can make people believe in anything."

The way people fell into The Veteran's scam was eloquent. It proves one of rhetoric's most uncomfortable truths: we are much more gullible and susceptible to manipulation than we'd like to admit. Any one of us could have been fooled by the backflips of their amphibious business partner. In some way or another, we all have been there.

In the Netflix documentary that bears his name, strategist Roger Stone said, "Truth? Who cares? Winning is all that matters." He took part in Donald Trump's first presidential campaign, staging several controversies.

Seconds later, he proudly said he was behind the story that Obama wasn't born in the United States. Although fake from its genesis, the story was very well suited to go viral. Social media disseminated it, and online trolls expanded and deepened its reach. It made it to the mainstream media, prime-time TV news and newspaper headlines.

The relationship between rhetoric and truth is a sensitive challenge of politics. Not for nothing has it been a central, long-dated topic of discussion. To exemplify this concept even further, let's look at Roger Stone's words, which echo the sophists who argue with Socrates in Plato's famous dialogue, Gorgias. The play's name honors one of the characters who was the most famous rhetorician of his time.

In that play, the sophist Callicles was a moral hardcore. For him, morality was a human construction opposed to nature. He claims that "true justice" is what nature taught us. The strong prevail over the weak. The aim of rhetoric, therefore, is to win, and it should be used for that purpose alone. Societal rules are mere shackles invented by the weak to constrain the strong. And one of those rules is telling the truth.

Plato admits that the sophist Protagoras enchanted the audience with his words. He compared Protagoras to the mythical Orpheus, as Socrates fell under his spell. He was "bewitched" for a long time and had to wait for the effect to pass. Only after the effects phased out did Socrates recover the power of his dialectical method.

The sophists established a renowned school in Athens. Their teachings were sought after from all over Greece. Their skepticism of established truths and focus on practicality made them political realists. They had no qualms about instrumentalizing profound aspects of human nature. Nor acknowledging power as life's ultimate (or perhaps only) goal. Gorgias, one of their most famous, amassed a fortune enough to commission a solid gold statue of himself. He left it at the Oracle of Delphi for posterity.

Furthermore, the sophists use reason and knowledge to satisfy personal and tribal interests. Under this logic, their mission was to help their clients gain power. They also serve different political factions for a fee. Not so different as today's communication consultants do.

In opposition to relativism, Plato set a sharp divide between knowledge and opinion. He proposed a clear distinction between the realm of science (*epistème*) and the realm of belief (*doxa*). This dichotomy formed the foundation of his ontology and epistemology, which determine reality and how we know it. From there, Plato addressed the inherent conflict between truth and politics.

While the sophists embraced relativism, Plato fought against it. He longed to reconstruct new criteria of thought and behavior that were immune to it. His solution, therefore, demanded a radical personal transformation. It was a "surgery of the soul" that removes our natural desires for self-affirmation and power. It entails a radicalism similar to that of Christians, Marxists or Shiites. And, like them, it pursues a new life ideal anchored in fixed principles and unwavering moral values.[37]

Ironically, Plato's extremism wasn't driven by pure ideals but by a practical concern. As W.K.C. Guthrie argued in his *History of Greek Philosophy*, Plato's works were always political.[38] The radicalism of his proposal was the only viable solution he saw for the polis of his time.

He came from an aristocratic family related to the famous Athenian lawmaker Solon. So, Plato was no stranger to power. His family belonged to the wealthiest and most politically active circles in Athens. His uncle Critias and cousin Charmides were part of the Thirty Tyrants government.

Plato's life was deeply intertwined with the tumultuous events of Athens. He witnessed the city's self-destruction. Political instability,

---

37 Rodríguez-Adrados, 1997.
38 Guthrie, 1979.

constant warfare, authoritarian rule, and demagogic manipulation became the rule. In these times, it wasn't just the city that seemed to crumble. An entire civilization appeared to be falling apart.

At the core of Plato's revolution lay a severe critique of rhetoric and its true power. He saw it as an irrational model of persuasion. It focuses on winning people's minds and hearts, not on the view that language reflects reality. This disregard for correspondence to truth was essential in Plato *and* the sophists. But while this was rhetoric's central deficit for him, it was one of its primary sources of power for them.

Plato's ideas gained traction in 4th-century BC Athens. But their actual impact became clear later. Stoicism and Epicureanism were more popular in the Hellenistic monarchies. And they maintained that status throughout the whole Roman Republic. However, Platonism surged again. This happened with the arrival of Christianity in the late Roman Empire. Its transcendent worldview resonated with the Christian faith. It offered similar responses to the uncertainties and ambiguities of human life.[39]

Platonism also offered a path to overcome the harsh realities of power politics. However, he avoided the mud of politics and truth. He did not try to untangle their knot. Instead, he proposed an ideal society from above. The polis he advocated for in *The Republic* was an aristocracy ruled by philosophers. Real ones, like Socrates or himself.

He never addressed, for example, the uncomfortable fact that truth, when inconvenient or unpopular, put at risk those who speak it. For a politician, this is a real danger. At the same time, lies and half-truths held greater power. That is why they are seen as not just helpful but justifiable, even necessary, in the political game. They are essential tools not just for demagogues but even for good politicians. As philosopher Hannah Arendt

---

39 Veyne, 2009.

summarized, while the truth's essence is to be impotent, it is in the very nature of power to be fallacious.[40]

Following Plato's footsteps, Arendt picked up the post left by him. But she did not give a solution based on how things should be. Instead, she approached the conflict between truth and politics from how things are. She started by raising a crucial question. Is it inherent to politics to achieve noble ends through dishonest means? Is truth destined to be excluded from the public sphere?

This led her to add another category to Plato's separation between doxa and episteme. She distinguished two sub-categories of epistemic truths. One is the rational truth of math and geometry, and the other is the factual truth of the concrete and empirical. While rational truths possess a solid resistance to power, factual truths don't.

They usually have a slight chance of surviving a direct confrontation with it. Power exceeds its dominion when it attacks rational truths. They have shown resilience, which is challenging to overcome, as it is often beyond its reach. But power fights on its ground when it falsifies or ignores facts.

In that sense, the recent phenomenon labelled as "post-truth" isn't entirely novel. Using distorted facts, half-truths, or lies have been age-old communication tactics, part of demagogy, propaganda, publicity, and public relations for as long as mankind has fought for power.

The difference is that the Internet made it easier to spread information – and misinformation. More and faster than ever before. The rise of 24-hour news cycles reshaped how news is produced and consumed. At the same time, social media platforms changed how people engage in discourse.

This shift grants individuals and groups a powerful megaphone to amplify their messages. Emotional overload, amplification and spin have

---

40 Arendt, 2017.

always competed with expert opinions and arguments. The Internet has simply tilted the playing field in favor of the former.

This media environment exacerbated a rhetorical duplicity in today's political communication. Especially in the democratic arena, political coalition campaigns show fiery exhalation when campaigning. However, as soon as they win, they change to a moderate, welcoming approach. As three-time New York Governor Mario Cuomo put it, "One campaigns in poetry but governs in prose."

This communicational change responds to the practicalities of governing. You need to deal with, manage, and align far more people. And they are more varied than those while campaigning. Not surprisingly, "to govern" comes from the Greek *kybernan*, a word of nautical origin "to steer a ship, to hold the helm, to pilot as a helmsman." To weather the currents and storms to bring the ship to port. To carry them all, for we are in the same boat.

But there is also an epistemological reason. Campaigning allows you to get higher up. You focus on ideals, values, and purposes. Yet, a firm grounding in facts is essential for effective government. Policymaking, law enforcement and economic management also depend heavily on reliable data. You need to get both the right facts and the facts right.

Now, distortion and vociferation have intensified. But so, too, has the demand for facts and data. Rather than a crisis, we are witnessing a diversification of truth. It may have waned in the mainstream media and front-line politics. They were eaten by the amoeban appeal of infotainment.

However, rational and factual knowledge are in great shape. They are in their respective technical and scientific realms. Research is more productive than ever, pushed by an unprecedented specialization of knowledge.

Today, our knowledge ranges from black holes the size of galaxies to the structure of genes. We have turned this understanding into millions of machines, devices and procedures. They are what "keeps modern society going," said Vaclav Smil. The resulting aggregated knowledge is immense. Far beyond the reach of any individual understanding.[41]

This is why, despite this vast knowledge pool, most of us lack a basic understanding of how our world works. We faintly know how our food, energy, and materials are produced. In that sense, Smil's book not only highlights the role of facts in comprehending our reality. It also shows the distance between scientific knowledge and our everyday understanding.

Our concept of truth is deeply intertwined with how our culture understands knowledge. It's not a truth handed down by gods. Nor held only by the elite, as some traditions believe.[42] Instead, it's a collective achievement built through systematic questioning and rigorous examination.

Plato's notion of objectivity is central to our understanding of truth. A widely accepted contemporary definition belongs to the so-called "correspondence theory." This defines truth as "the correspondence of language or thought to a mind-independent world."[43] In other words, truth is an alignment of language with an objective reality. That means one that exists independently of our minds. Therefore, truth occurs when our words and ideas accurately reflect the world around us.[44]

The problem is that not all the forms of human language are appropriate to the task. Plato recognized this early. He saw that natural language was too open to be having many meanings and the influence of power. As for the language of politics, dominated by rhetoric, is full of vested interest to be trusted. That concern added to the need for objectivity as a core condition of the scientific method.

---

41 Smil, 2022.

42 Baggini, 2018.

43 Stanford Encyclopedia of Philosophy, 2024.

44 Merriam Webster, 2024.

Over the centuries, empirical facts became the building blocks of this approach. This consolidated the need for rigorous testing and its corresponding use of assertions. The latter ended up being the natural expression of facts.

In that sense, setting a clear line between science and non-science was also Plato's legacy. His separation didn't admit graduality and left no room for a grey area. This mandate for objectivity, reliance on empirical facts and separation between science and non-science became ingrained in Western scientific thought. Karl Popper's work on distinguishing science from pseudoscience was part of this tradition.

Scientists consider this line a sharp and impassable divide. For those who know or work with the scientific method, there's no room for ambiguity. It's either demonstrably true through rigorous testing or simply it isn't science.

In contrast, people who are not scientists are not aware of this divide. The less educated and educated-but-not-smart tend to be devoted believers. The world is full of beings and entities, all of which there is no evidence of their existence. There is a wide variety: ghosts, UFOs, angels, demons, tarot, the Chupacabra, Reiki, Sasquatch, and flat-earthers. There are hybrids, too. Some look like moles or lizards walking among us in disguise. They pretend to be world leaders, Hollywood stars, or British royals.

The epistemology of facts and truth determines their rhetorical possibilities and uses. Epistemic knowledge uses language, and, as such, it has a rhetoric, too. This leads us to delve into the role of facts as rhetorical devices.

First, objectivity exerts a significant influence in shaping our perception of truth. As it makes truth look and sound more valid, objectivity is where veracity comes from.

Second, similar to how judgment can pose different degrees of plausibility, assertions can also vary in the truth they commit. Generally, the more empirical an assertion is, the better. This is because the more factual it is, the easier it is to include particular details, like names, dates, locations, and numbers.

On the linguistic front, this empirical quality is expressed through specificity. The more referential details an assertion contains, the greater its veracity. That veracity is epistemological but also rhetorical. Therefore, it depends on how those referential details are presented (See Table 31.)

TABLE 31:

ASSERTIONS / CASE 1	N	Q	D	%
(a) Others have transferred the price raise directly to their clients and profits have not fallen	X	X	X	X
(b) **Vinovio Ltd.** transferred the price raise directly to its clients, and its profits have not fallen	✓	X	X	X
(c) **Six months** ago, **Vinovio Ltd.** transferred the increase directly to its clients, and its profits have not fallen.	✓	✓	✓	X
(d) **Six months** ago, **Vinovio Ltd.** transferred the increase directly to **80%** of its clients, and its profits have not fallen.	✓	✓	✓	✓
ASSERTIONS / CASE 2	N	Q	D	%
(a) In some mountains, most accidents occurred during descent because it snowed regularly at noon.	X	X	X	X
(b) In the **Cordillera Real,** most accidents occurred during descent because it snowed regularly at noon.	✓	X	X	X
(c) In the last **decade** at **Cordillera Real,** most accidents occurred during descent because it snowed regularly at noon on more than **300 days** a year on average.	✓	✓	✓	X
(d) In the last **decade** at **Cordillera Real**, more than **90%** of accidents occurred during descent as it snowed regularly between **11am** and **3pm**, on an average of more than **300 days a year**.	✓	✓	✓	✓

To sound truthful, a message needs to be plausible for the audience. This means aligning with what they already understand or can be convinced of through solid evidence. Based on the available evidence, the speaker's job is to calibrate the message's intensity.

One effective way to achieve this is by using modal verbs. These verbs, like "can," "could," "may," "might," "shall," "should," "will," and "would," modify the action of the main verb. They add nuance and indicate the level of certainty associated with the message. This maintains syntactic simplicity, which is crucial for a strategic message's clarity.

Let's return to section 3.2 (page 72,) where Patagonia's activism team meets the minister of energy to get him to agree to publicly criticize the dam project. As we saw in that case, Patagonia's activism manager might say, "Publicly criticizing the dam project will make you popular with young people." While seemingly straightforward, this judgment can be expressed with varying degrees of certainty (as illustrated in Table 32.)

By incorporating modal verbs, Patagonia's activism team can tailor the message's strength to the evidence they possess. They might choose:

TABLE 32:

SUBJECT	VERB	OBJECT	MODE
Criticizing the project	will make you (1) makes you (2) would make you (3) may make you (4) could make you (5)	popular with young people	(1) *Future indicative* (2) *Present indicative* (3) *Conditional* (4) *Modal verb "may"* (5) *Modal verb "could"*

Judgments, by their very nature, are not simply true or false. They are, in fact, either well-founded or not. This distinction is essential as it highlights the nuanced nature of critical thinking. A well-founded judgment is supported by a valid, evidence-based assertion. When it is not well-funded, it lacks this crucial support.

Understanding the relationship between judgments and assertions is vital. Judgments, on their own, lack veracity. However, they gain credibility when supported by a veracious assertion. This dynamic is exemplified in the following extract from The Economist, a publication known for applying those principles.

> *Men Adrift: Badly educated men in rich countries have not adapted well to trade, technology, or feminism.*
>
> *Unskilled men have less to offer than once they did. First, women are now better educated than men; the proportion of women with no more than a high-school education fell from 32.9% in 1979— one percentage point higher than men—to 11.4% in 2013, one percentage point lower.*
>
> *Second, many men do not work at all. In America, the share of men of prime working age who have a job has fallen from a peak of nearly 95% in the mid-1960s to only 84% in 2010. In Britain, the share of men aged 16-64 who work has fallen from 92% in 1971 to 76% in 2013; for women it has risen from 53% to 67%.*
>
> *[...] [Today] 23% of married American women with children now out-earn their husbands, up from 4% in 1960. Few women in rich countries now need a man's support to raise a family.*
>
> THE ECONOMIST, MAY 28, 2015.

The Economist takes special care in supporting ideas with arguments and facts. That rigorous support allows the magazine to deliver its ideas through strong judgments. In fact, the key messages of its articles are usually insightful statements. This is the case with "Badly educated men in rich countries are adrift."

These judgments then receive support from further judgments (2), (3), and (4). They also act as topic sentences, briefly summarizing the supporting arguments. Each supporting judgment is bolstered by evidence-based assertions (i), (ii), (iii), and (iv).

TABLE 33

STRUCTURE			Function	Speech Act
1. Badly educated men in rich countries are adrift			Key message	Judgment
↓	↓	↓	Arguments Topic Sentences	Judgments
2. Women are now better educated than men.	3. Many men do not work at all	4. Few women in rich countries now need a man's support to raise a family.		
↓	↓	↓	Evidence	Supporting Assertions
(i) The proportion of women with no more than a high-school education fell from 32.9% in 1979—one percentage point higher than men—to 11.4% in 2013, one percentage point lower.	(ii) In America, the share of men of prime working age who have a job has fallen from a peak of nearly 95% in the mid-1960s to only 84% in 2010.	(iii) [Today] 23% of married American women with children now out-earn their husbands, up from 4% in 1960.		
(iv) In Britain the share of men aged 16-64 who work has fallen from 92% in 1971 to 76% in 2013; for women it has risen from 53% to 67%.				

It is not that The Economist doesn't have a political stance. It does, and a partisan one, stating its political leanings and preferred candidates. The editors self-identify as "radical centrists," championing free trade, globalization, and open markets.

The magazine's style has been described as 'data journalism' and 'interpretative analysis.' Its sensemaking method involves meticulous data analysis and interpretation. This has also proven to be well-suited for smart, educated audiences. Or for a readership of "prominent business leaders and policymakers," the magazine boasts.

Some have suggested that this kind of journalism is outmoded. Brexit, which the Economist was vocally against, would express that. Tabloids like The Daily Mail supported Brexit and won, while The Economist lost. But that has more to do with its political stance than the writing style.

Whatever the case, combining insightful perspectives with hard facts is a worthwhile practice. It harnesses persuasive power. It also improves our critical vision and explanatory flair. It helps us see the big picture of complex things.

We have examined how judgments and assertions each have a regulating mechanism of their own. Judgments can be stronger by changing the verb. Assertions can be truer by adding details.

Still, judgements and assertions are complementary. Their logics work together. The stronger the evidence supporting a claim, the more emphatic the judgment becomes. Conversely, weaker evidence leads to less assertive judgments. Let us see how this applies to another case previously presented in this book. We'll return to Ismene, the winery's export manager of section 2.2.2. (page 57.) She needed to convince British wine distributor Malcolm to accept a price increase. Suppose she knew that the distribution companies Vinovio and Wineco maintained their profits. They did so despite passing the wine's price increase to their customers six months ago.

If there is evidence, the judgment could be, "The price increase won't affect your profits." However, if the only evidence comes from a small distributor in Wales, the message must be more cautious. It should mitigate the extent of what it says. In this case, a less assertive one. "An increase does not have to affect profits" would better fit the weaker evidence. The following table presents this case with two other examples (See Table 34.)

TABLE 34

JUDGEMENT (RHET. STRENGTH)	ASSERTIONS (VERACITY)
The price increase **won't** affect your profits (high).	[because] **Six months** ago, **Vinovio and Wineco** transferred the increase directly to their clients and their profits have not fallen. (+)
The price increase **does not have** to affect your profits (low).	[because] Other distributors transferred the price increase directly to its clients and their profits have not fallen. (-)
Criticizing the dam **will** make you popular with young people.	[because] More than **80%** of adults between **18** and **30** oppose the dam project, according to the latest **Gallup, IPSUM** and **INSUC** surveys
Criticizing the dam **could** make you popular with young people.	[because] Polls and surveys have shown that most young people oppose the dam project.
Start walking at 2am **may/could** help us reach the summit and return safely.	In the last **decade** at Andes' **Cordillera Real** more than **90%** of accidents occurred during descent as it snowed regularly between **11am** and **3pm**, on an average of more than **300 days** per year.
Starting to walk at 2am **will** help us reach the summit and return safely.	In the **Andes** mountains most accidents occurred during descent as it snowed regularly at noon.

Thus, the more evidence we have, the more assertive our message can be. Likewise, the less evidence we have, the more moderate our message, and the weaker it must be. Let us look at the example in Graph 1. Statement

A.1 says as follows. "In the last Index national survey, 95% of adults aged 18 to 30 said their top worry is protecting the environment." Here, the evidence we have is divergent to the dam project. Yet, it still makes it reasonable to say M1. "Publicly criticizing the dam project could increase your popularity among young people."

However, this changes if, in addition to this, we have two more evidence-providing assertions (A.2 and A.3.) Thus, a moderate judgment like M.1 misses the opportunity to deliver a more powerful message. Indeed, if the three assertions A.1, A.2, and A.3 support the message. Then, the potential benefit can be expressed sharper (and more probable.) That is the case of M.3: "Publicly criticizing the dam project will make you a rockstar to young people" (see Graph 1.)

GRAPH 1

(+)

>>
VE
RA
CI
TY
>>

(-)

(M.1) "Publicly criticizing the dam project could make you more popular among young people."

[because] (A.1) "In the latest Index national survey, 95% of adults between 18 and 30 stated that their greatest concern is protecting the environment."

(M.2) "Publicly criticizing the dam project will make you more popular among young people."

[because] (A.1) "In the latest Index national survey, 95% of adults between the ages of 18 and 30 stated that their greatest concern is protecting the environment."

(A.2) "More than 80% of adults between 18 and 30 oppose the dam project according to the latest IPSUM, CEP and INSUC surveys.

(M.3) "Publicly criticizing the dam project will make you a rockstar to young people."

[because] (A.1) ""In the latest Index national survey, 95% of adults between 18 and 30 stated that their greatest concern is protecting the environment."

(A.2) " More than 80% of adults between 18 and 30 oppose the dam project, according to the latest IPSUM, CEP and INSUC surveys."

(A.3) "At the beginning of this month, between 250,000 and 350,000 people – mostly young adults – participated in a march down the streets, protesting the project."

(–) >> INTENTIONALITY OF THE MESSAGE >> (+)

The interaction between evidence and the message's intensity is a powerful rhetorical tool. It allows us to synergically combine meaning and truth. "One of the key skills of great presenters," states Nancy Duarte, is that they can combine "story and data like layers of a cake."[45]

4.2. The license of ethos

Along with evidence, the speaker's ethos is another element that affects the message. Factual evidence is subject to a plurality of views and disputes over significance. It is also vulnerable to the interference of power and the "spell" of rhetoric, which ethos is part of.

However, along with its rhetorical capacity as a source of Aristotelian deliberative persuasion, ethos could also work as an identity driver for tribal rhetoric. The original word has a double meaning in ancient Greek: on the one hand, it means "character" (ἦθος) and, on the other, "habit" (εθος). This origin refers to a speaker's permanent quality, a recognized "recognized way of being" *(hexis)*. So, it also belongs to the realm of action, perceived behavior and being. In fact, both words "ethology," which is the study of the behavior of non-human animals, and "ethics," which has been defined as theory of human life, come from ethos.[46] Ethics is the realm of human actions and its social legitimacy. It considers whether these are right or wrong. It examines how they align with a set of beliefs and values.

This inevitably leads to culture and identity. Besides convincing others, rhetoric's essential function is reinforcing "us" against the "others." The goal is to build, invigorate, and strengthen a group's sense of belonging. This is why a strong ethos can overcome opposing facts.

Donald Trump's political success is a good example. In 2017, he took office as president of the United States. Whether you like him or not, you

---

45 Duarte, 2008.
46 Stanford Encyclopedia of Philosophy, 2018.

cannot deny his significance as a political landmark. Trump has repeatedly and publicly shown little respect for facts. He lies, contradicts himself, and denies taking actions recorded on video. Yet, one of history's most democratic nations elected him. A democracy that is also the most hegemonic power ever. This is a milestone in history. This was when the United States also became a model for the post-truth era.

Trump's communication was strategic. It appealed to the fears and anxieties of a tribe: white Americans without a college degree, often called the "white working class." Any clear tribal profile is easy to manipulate, and it is especially so when an underlying fact fuels it. Indeed, the American white working class has suffered a decline. Their quality of life and social capital have fallen more than any other relative group. Economists Ann Case and Angus Deaton[47] have studied and documented this. Between 1999 and 2013, there was a significant increase in mortality among middle-aged non-Hispanic whites. This change reversed decades of improvements in mortality. It was also unique to the United States. No other wealthy country has experienced a similar change.

To a certain degree, this was a consequence of globalization and policymaking. Many measures may have helped the entire country's economy. But they hurt the traditional institutions that provided social capital. This was especially true for the white working class. Social capital is not a market factor. It is crucial to people's well-being and fundamental to their sense of belonging.

At the same time, the liberal left was winning one cultural battle after another. It has been relentless in the early 21st Century. It has pushed its issues onto the mainstream agenda with a determination that went from assertive to intolerant. This widened the gap between facts and discourse. This made conservative groups distrust the liberal media and fueled

---

47 Case & Deaton, 2015.

polarization. Over the months, a tribe's identity was fully consolidated. And with that, a reinforced "spiral of silence" grew in former moderates. This phenomenon was key to Donald Trump's triumph and the "leave" vote in the Brexit referendum.

Some analysts called 2016 the "year of the popular revolt." Many people voted against the political elites and the mainstream media. The National Academy of Sciences (NAS) conducted a study on this. It found that the white working class voted for Trump because they fear "cultural displacement." They feared a threat to their dominant cultural status over the country.[48]

By the time the liberal elite realized this, it was too late. The tribe that supported Trump was immune to liberal speech or logos. Instead of addressing that group's needs, frustrations, and fears, the liberal elite did the opposite. It deepened their commitment to a progressive agenda. Then, in the white working-class tribe's eyes, they had become the abominable liberal media.

The Democratic campaign sought to attack Trump's ethos. But they could not land a blow. They may have been self-focused. Because of this, they failed to see, early enough, Trump's source of credibility. He had credibility with his target audience, not the audience of democrat hipsters. Thus, the elite Democrats attacked him first for being a sexual predator and harasser. Second, for hating immigrants. Neither attack had any effect. This is because his white audience did not find these things problematic. For them, he was and is, first and foremost, a successful businessman and entrepreneur. He is an outsider in politics and an ordinary man—like them.

Trump is a master communicator. He skillfully restated his ethos with seriousness. It was based on self-confidence. He repeatedly said nobody would own him, saying, "I don't need anyone's money. I use my own

---

48 Jones et al., 2017.

money. I'm not using the lobbyists. I'm not using donors. I don't care."[49] Wall Street-owned Obama and the Clintons do not understand economics. They were always public servants. Trump could "make it" in America instead. That is precisely the source of credibility that supports his ethos. Once in office, he introduced himself to the world as President on the White House website as follows:

Donald Trump is the very definition of the American Success story.

Throughout his life, he has continually set the standards of business and entrepreneurial excellence, especially with his interests in real estate, sports, and entertainment.

Likewise, his entry into politics resulted in the Presidential victory in, miraculously, his first-ever run for office.

The White House.

In that sense, the ethos' source of credibility becomes evident in the context of the values system of a given community or culture. That's why, as a strategic variable, ethos transcends and underpins explicit discourse. It can influence the intensity of the message and its need for evidence in a structured manner. This makes it possible to establish the following pattern: The greater my ethos, the more force I can lend to my message. Consequently, the lesser the ethos, the lesser the intensity. This mutual reinforcement relationship corresponds to a system dynamic's *"reinforcing loop."*[50]

Therefore, the greater my ethos, the less evidence I need. The less credible my ethos, the more evidence I need. This relationship is not one of mutual reinforcement but of joint balance. This corresponds to the system dynamic's *balancing loop* (see Figure 15 and Table 35.)

---

49 Político, 2015.
50 Sterman, 2000.

TABLE 35:

RELATIONS		
Message's strength	Ethos credibility	Need for evidence
High +	High +	Low -
Low -	Low -	High +
Message <=> Ethos (+) Mutual reinforcement		Ethos <=> Evidence (–) Mutual balance

FIGURE 15:

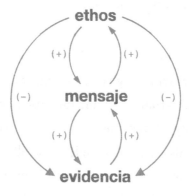

An example from the financial industry clarifies this. Warren Buffett and Jordan Belfort, the "Wolf of Wall Street," need evidence differently. So does their ethos's license for the intensity of their messages. Warren Buffett is a highly credible investor. He does not need to present much evidence. He can even do without it, especially in the case of moderate messages.

Jordan Belfort's credibility, on the contrary, is low. He can only be convincing if he has enough evidence, even for the most moderate messages. Conversely, he cannot deliver more assertive messages, even with evidence. His level of credibility does not allow it (see Table 36.)

TABLE 36

Warren Buffett		ETHOS	Jordan Belfort
CREDIBILITY	POWER OF THE MESSAGE		CREDIBILITY
Evidence + 2	1. Invest in cryptocurrencies now		X
Evidence + 1	3. You should invest in cryptocurrencies		X
✓	2. Cryptocurrencies can be a good investment		Evidence + 3
✓	4. Some cryptocurrencies could become a good investment.		Evidence + 1

Aristotle said that audiences follow the trustworthy speaker. They do it "most readily and quickly on almost all subjects." And entirely so in affairs in which there are no exact criteria (to decide the case,) but only wavering opinions (*Rhet.* I.2, 1356a6–8.)

Without other decision criteria, the audience can judge based on the speaker's suggestions. Yet, this works if it's deemed acceptable and trustworthy (which it will be if their ethos with their audience is strong.)

In this way, we can see how the importance of ethos grows. This is especially true in matters of opinion, which cannot be resolved with evidence. They inevitably remain open to interpretation or doubt. In short, a speaker's credibility is tied to the intensity of the message, the evidence, and their understanding of the audience.

Once you have identified these elements and relationships, you calibrate the message accordingly. Let us continue with the example of the export manager who must raise the price of their flagship wine to the British distributor. The exporter manager has a strong ethos. It is based on a relationship of mutual trust after ten years of doing business together.

Also, on the global reach and reputation of the wine company. In that case, the export manager could state that the price increase "will not affect your profit." But, if he is not credible, the assertive message may trigger distrust or skepticism in the British distributor. Instead, he should present only a probability, such as the price increase "may not harm your profit." It's much safer (see Figure 16.)

FIGURE 16:

16.1. BUILD THE MESSAGE:

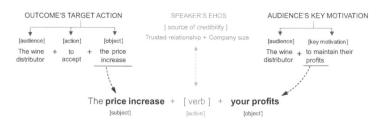

16.2. CALIBRATE THE MESSAGE:

KEY TAKEAWAYS OF CHAPTER 4

➢ Truthfulness and credibility are essential for persuasive communication.

➢ Messages should be plausible and aligned with the audience's understanding or supported by strong evidence.

➢ Judgments and assertions work together. Judgments provide meaning and direction, while assertions provide factual support.

➢ Cultural context and shared knowledge matter. Tailor messages to the audience's cultural background and understanding.

➢ Modal verbs calibrate message intensity. Use modal verbs to indicate the level of certainty associated with the message.

➢ Ethos influences message strength. The more credible the speaker, the more assertive the message can be.

STEP 5

MAKING IT REAL

This chapter focuses on the execution of strategic messaging. It discusses the distinction between messages and slogans, highlighting their different rhetorical purposes and levels of referentiality. The text also explores the role of judgments and assertions in conveying truth and credibility, emphasizing the need for well-founded judgments supported by factual assertions. Additionally, it delves into the challenges and opportunities presented by the digital age and the rise of mass self-communication, highlighting the importance of crafting messages that resonate with diverse audiences and withstand scrutiny in the public sphere.

STEPS:

1. Think first, then plan.

2. Find the hinges: target action and key motivation.

3. Do the magic: build the message through an equation.

4. Bring that support: calibrate evidence and ethos.

5. **Making it real: prepare the execution.**

Now that we have set all the key elements of the messaging, we need to plan how it will be executed. This is of capital importance. Many races are lost in the last seconds, and ascents fail a few meters from reaching the summit. It's the same with messaging.

Of course, here, the last bit is the actual physical execution. Nonverbal signals are essential to communication in sound, image, or presence. Most experts agree that nonverbal communication can convey more meaning than verbal. Some even argue that it often accounts for two-thirds of all communications. This applies to phone calls, speeches, and presentations. It also applies to meetings, audio messages, and face-to-face conversations.

This is why politicians, business leaders, and public figures seek acting training. They also seek coaching from professionals. They must master or at least control their body language. The message is framed by their voice, eye contact, expressions, gestures, and posture. A good actor makes a massive difference in a play or movie. And bad acting can quickly spoil a good story. Imagine if Martin Scorsese had chosen Steven Segal, not young Robert De Niro, as the *Taxi Driver*.

However, there is another critical step before performing. It means reordering the parts of the messaging process. These parts are the message, evidence, and credentials in an execution's "script." The reason for this is that message-building follows an order. This order is only sometimes the best for execution. The message has five steps. First, set the strategy. Second, find the hinges. Third, build the message. Fourth, provide evidence. Finally, tune the message and pick ethos' credentials.

The importance of the script cannot be underestimated. As filmmaker Akira Kurosawa said: "A good script can make a masterpiece with a good director. But, with the same script, a mediocre director can make a passable film. But with a lousy script, even a good director can't possibly make a good film."

Likewise, deficient content can seriously undermine even a nonverbal communication master.

It could harm their ethos, as with people recognized for speaking nonsense beautifully.

5.1. A message, not a slogan

The Cambridge Dictionary defines a *message* as "information communicated to somebody."[51] For example, "She's not here. Do you want to leave her a *message?*" The term comes from the Latin word *missus*, which means "sending away, dispatching; a throwing, hurling". This, in turn, comes from the past participle of *mittere*, "to release, let go; send, throw."

Yet, a message also means "the intended meaning or significance of something." This is more like "They didn't get the message; they're not interested. In that sense, a message has a core communicational/cognitive aspiration. This is why it is intrinsically pressured to be explicit, direct, and clear. It should not be symbolic, tacit, coded, or ambiguous. If so, we are no longer talking about a message but an epigram, aphorism, proverb, poem, or slogan.

In contrast to a message, a slogan is "a short phrase that is easy to remember and is used to make people notice something."[52] The term comes from the Gaelic word *sluagh-ghairm*, which means "war cry" and refers to a clan motto in the face of battle. In the Middle Ages, slogans served as passwords. They ensured recognition at night or in battle chaos.[53] Since the beginning of the 18th Century, the word (as *slughon*) took on its metaphorical sense. It meant "a distinctive word or phrase used by a political or other group."

Messages and slogans also diverge in their rhetorical natures. According to Aristotle, rhetoric has three distinctive genres. They differ not only in object but also in purpose. First, there is *deliberative* rhetoric,

---

51 The Cambridge Dictionary, 2022
52 Idem
53 Denton, 1980.

which is about *what to do*. Oriented towards decision-making, it deals with the uncertainty of the future. Therefore, their object is prospective facts and their relationship with today's actions.

This is the rhetoric used by the Athenians to discuss matters of the *polis* or city-state. Same as today's political and business leaders. What should we do? Do we declare war on Sparta or not? Do we raise or lower taxes on companies? Do we implement SAP this year? Should we vote for this mayor candidate or another? Do we strengthen the face-to-face channel with our customers or focus on the digital channel?

Second, there is *judicial* rhetoric. Its objects are mainly past facts. It is typical of the court, market, and news. Did you run the fence off the property? Did you drive with alcohol? How many clay statues did you ship? Did you pay the agreed price for the service? When did the economy stop defaulting? Currently, messages are widely used in both deliberative and judicial rhetoric. They are the intended meaning or significance communicated to somebody.

However, Aristotle also distinguished a third rhetoric genre. He named it *ceremonial* or *epideictic*. This genre promotes virtues or criticizes vices, usually of a person. It presents facts to an audience that cannot influence them. They could only agree or disagree with the speaker's praise or critique. It was used in ceremonies or commemorations. These include marriages, funerals, or festivals (like the Olympic Games.) This also includes state visits and other formal events.

For this type of speech, the speaker should focus on what the audience wants. At the same time, the audience suspends its commitment to truth. They do this in mutual agreement with the speaker. For example, at funerals, it is expected that "no one speaks ill of the dead."

Aristotle considered ceremonial rhetoric the least profound of the three genres. He spent less time and effort analyzing and explaining

WORDS THAT GET RESULTS

it.[54] Maybe it was because he found it less challenging. As he himself put it, recalling a phrase from Socrates: "It is not hard to praise the Athenians in Athens" (*Ret* 1358b). In any case, the imbalance was notorious. It made people see ceremonial rhetoric as more style than substance, which is partly true.

This less important role attributed to ceremonial rhetoric would change dramatically with the arrival of modern mass media. The rich and powerful always sought to convey their messages through monuments, epitaphs, or sculptures. However, their scope was limited before printing. With the birth of the newspaper and current news in the 17th century, their messages could reach millions.[55] Modern advertising and propaganda were born.

But what unleashed ceremonial rhetoric's boom was its association with the 20th century's mass media through marketing and advertising. Much like propaganda, the success of traditional advertising depended mainly on controlling the message. This is why mass media and 20[th-]century authoritarian regimes got along so well. It was as if they were meant to each other. A wannabe totalitarian state meets a media system that has a natural tendency towards centralization. Thus, we had Hitler, Stalin, Franco, Ceausescu, Gaddafi, Pol-Pot, Pinochet, and Kim Jong-Il, among others.

Without mass media, the rise of Fascism, National Socialism, Stalinism, or Maoism would have been more challenging. However, they encountered mass media that offered a real chance to impose their messages. To make society a captive audience of political power. Once it took over the media, it was almost impossible to dispute the official narrative.

In 1933, the father of American public relations, Edward Bernays recognized the Nazis were using his techniques. He published *Crystallizing Public Opinion* (1928) and *Propaganda* (1928), which became instant

---

54 Lockwood, 1996.
55 Pettegree, 2014.

classics. Now, the Third Reich was using his ideas and principles in their campaign against the Jews.

Four years later, in 1937, sales guru Elmer Wheeler published *Tested Sentences that Sell*. It was ground-breaking and quickly became a marketing classic. That same year, Joseph Stalin initiated the Great Purge to consolidate his power over the Soviet state. Adolf Hitler secretly met with his military and foreign policy captains in Germany. He shared his expansive plans to recover "living space" for the German people.

In his book, Wheeler gave three pieces of advice. They are now modern marketing must. First, "Do not sell the steak; sell the sizzle." This refers to the idea that we should focus on the most remarkable attraction. It could be an image or sound. Anything that triggers our senses and can lead our clients to buy. Second, "the first ten words matter more than the next ten thousand." Be brief and precise. The masses judge quickly and do not want to waste time. Third, "win decisions, not arguments." If the customer objects, don't waste time in the argument. Instead, give the reason and lead them from the benefit of the product to the sizzle.[56] Simplicity, brevity, and superficiality define old advertising. They were the key to its 20th-century success.

As modern versions of ceremonial rhetoric, marketing and advertising exclude potential nuances. This omission becomes mandatory for spreading ads in newspapers, magazines, radio and television. It rapidly colonized the media realm worldwide and then jumped to the public space to become ubiquitous today.

On the night of August 31st, 1939, Germany staged a false attack on its radio station, Sender Gleiwitz. Hitler then used it as a *casus bello* to the invasion of Poland, which started the following day. That event initiated WWII and was a farce planned, manufactured, and orchestrated by Göebbels. Then, the Germans spread false news to the media (which he controlled.)

---

56 Thompson, 2017.

In a market democracy, the mass media system also favors controlling the message. First, it has a natural tendency to form oligopolies. Second, its channels are unidirectional. They go from one to many, one way only. Also, mass media have higher production and distribution costs than their pre-modern predecessors. Their price is also substantially higher than their Internet-based post-modern successors.

In a mass media society, a company or politician hires an agency to craft a message. Then, the agency spreads it through the selected media to thousands or millions. People may indeed choose whether to buy or not. But they cannot publicly dispute the message's truth or meaning. Whether on television or the radio, at the cinema or in the newspaper, you are at the receiving end. Always.

However, now, the mass media system of the mid-20th century overlaps with the *late* 20th-century media system. Yet, the Internet cannot be compared to a particular medium in its different applications. Like an electrical network, it is a digital, interactive, and complex hypertext fabric. Spanish sociologist Manuel Castells named it mass *self-communication*.[57]

The Internet offers a new space for public debate and the struggle for meaning. It gives our leaders the power to install an idea and reach 10 million minds worldwide in a millisecond.[58] It offers the same to its competitors and opponents, as well as to the 10 million citizens who receive its original message.

Throughout history, new media technologies have usually produced significant social transformations. This is particularly true when the new media changes who can create and spread content and meaning.[59]

57 Castells, 2009.
58 Thompson, 2016.
59 Kress, 2005.

Today, audiences can be creators. The former passive receiver of media messages can now object the truth, question honesty, or dispute its meaning. And reach millions through their social networks.

Digital technologies, mobile phones, and access to the Internet have spread worldwide. That has imposed new challenges for traditional sources of power and means of control. Authoritarian regimes still insist on taking over the media. It may be more challenging and costly, but it is still possible. You can seize all the infrastructure: buildings, offices, antennas, TV studios, radio stations, etc. Controlling the message, however, is far more complex. You cannot capture the entire Internet.[60]

All this has made ceremonial rhetoric much more vulnerable to facts. Regarding truth and veracity, ceremonial rhetoric has always played in a separate, sheltered field. Quite uneven in its favor. Now, confronted in a more even ring, ceremonial rhetoric is not good at resisting blows from factual truths. It crumbles easily. It is as if, at a funeral, the disruptive relative who whispers jokes about the deceased now would share the pulpit and microphone with the priest.

The vulnerability of ceremonial rhetoric caused the standard marketing discourse to lose credibility. The effects may be more profound than they seem.

In much of the English and Spanish-speaking world, "that's pure marketing" means "that's not true." So, for at least an outreach to 20% of the world's population, "marketing" is an exchangeable word for bogus or phony. This suggests a demise in marketing's predominance as the way of communicating value. It may correlate to the rise and fall of mass media.

---

60 The exception to the rule may be China, North Korea, Cuba or Venezuela, but it's not like you can email them and simply ask. The last remnants of communism have somewhat successfully highjacked the Internet, to the point that they limit connectivity and control the information shared online. But as we said before, they're the exception to the rule, proving the rule true for the rest of the world. The alternative realities of the communist countries are the last attempt to keep alive a dying model of power and control through mass communication.

The other key difference distinguishing a message from a slogan is its referentiality. This is the capacity of a piece of language to refer to concrete and objective entities of the world.

For example, in the following sentences, the statement gains referentiality. You can see this as you go from sentence (a) to sentence (c) (see Table 37):

a) "Someone close to me had an awful experience in the restaurant of an acquaintance."

b) "A close family member became intoxicated in the restaurant of a common relative."

c) "My brother got food poisoning from an oyster in our cousin's bistro."

TABLE 37

	REFERENTS		
Semantical	Agent	Action	Object / Mode / Circumstance
Syntactical	Subject	Verb	Complement
(a)	Someone close	Had an awful experience.	The restaurant of an acquaintance
(b)	A close family member	Got intoxicated.	The restaurant of a common relative
(c)	My brother	Got food poisoning from an oyster	Our cousin's bistro

The statement gains referentiality in the following four elements: *agent*, *action*, *object*, and *mode*. In that order, these elements align with the sentence parts: *subject*, *verb*, and *complement*. Usually, the agent is the subject. The verb shows the action. The object, mode, or other information is one or more complements. The rule for them all is that the more specific they refer to, the more *referential* the sentence is.

There are two human domains in which language must have sound referentiality. Generally seen as opposites, these domains are science and storytelling.

People who know how to tell stories use *vivid* language. It means referring to individual objects and actions in a particular time-space frame. This leads the reader to form images and even imagine scenes. This is partly what Henry James and Ernest Hemingway meant. They said writers should "show, not tell." They must *show* events and situations with material and physical details to appeal to our senses. In that way, the audience can *experience* the story. Storytelling loses its essence and power if the speech explains too much. Or if the references are too abstract.

Narratives can also be deployed as reports. The main difference is that reporting seeks —and promises— objectivity. In modern democracies, our understanding of the world starts with journalists. They are who show us current affairs. We can then go deeper into almost any subject by accessing reports and studies usually provided by experts. Also, by public institutions or civil society organizations. Finally, science offers one further step. It has the most definite word about how things are.

Scientific writing reinforces referentiality on two levels. First, it reports, like journalism, what happened. It refers to tests, experiments, modelling, and results. They occurred at a specific time and place. Thus, they become assertions with past tense verbs when incorporated into the paper. As such, the more particularity they have, the more veracity they provide. [61]

---

61 In essence, modern science uses written format. Thus, it must follow a specific set of linguistic rules that facilitate the production and sharing of scientific knowledge. It is true that throughout history, experts and scholars have also used the oral and visual, too. However, most coding, transmitting, and stockpiling has been done in writing. In fragments, treatises, books, or letters -- like the ones Newton read from Galileo and Kepler. This process consolidated in the first half of the 20th century. It did so by converging the format and style of science almost exclusively in what we now call research articles or papers.

On another level, science reinforces the referentiality of abstractions. This is anchored in the deep-rooted platonic idea of objectivity as a condition for truth. To do so, scientific rhetoric tightens its semantic universe. It does that by changing the linguistic expression of its objects from *words* to *terms*.[62]

This is why research is essential for both the writer and the scientist. Their crafts involve knowing the world to which they refer. It could be the first-person experience of a neurosurgeon, like in Ian McEwan's novel *Saturday* (2005). Or, in the scientist's case, the state of the discipline in which research is built up. In sum, all the relevant writing that has been researched and published lately.

They should know the critical parts of that world —objects, actions, qualities, and relationships. The more I know, the deeper I can go. Today, Chat GPT and other AI assistants can add referentiality by providing facts, cases, and details. However, the addition is ex-post. It cannot counter the shallowness of being thought and conceived from a poorer, lesser-experienced world. Without a thorough reference, a message is always at risk of saying something vague, wrong, or nothing at all.

While messages seek to be highly referential, slogans do not. They are expected to deliberately omit it or blur the reference for the sake of their rhetorical gimmick. The following table compares the referentiality of different types of slogans and messages. Some are maxims, famous phrases, and even corporate definitions (see Table 38.)

---

62 A word can mean many things. It is open to polysemy. For example, *"function"* can mean a natural purpose. Like, "a sea current's function is to redistribute heat." Or it can mean a person's duty. For instance, "my function in our team is reducing costs." Or it can mean a ceremony. "She has to attend two official functions." But, in math, *function* means just one thing. It is "an operation that relates one variable to one or more other variables." An unequivocal referent within a particular disciplinary field. Same case with terms used in biology or chemistry.

TABLE 38

MESSAGES: SAYINGS, QUOTES, DEFINITIONS	SLOGAN
No exchange takes place in a free market unless both parties' benefit. (Friedman, 1981)	There's no free lunch.
A man is a wolf rather than a man to whom is a stranger. (Plautus, 208 B.C.)	Man's wolf to man.
Making your wife happy helps to make your life much happier. (Anonymous)	Happy wife happy life.
News is what somebody does, not want you to print. All the rest is advertising. (Anonymous)	Democracy dies in darkness
Our purpose is opening up a world of opportunity. (Purpose statement, HSBC)	The world's local bank.
To be a leading global premium and luxury wine brand. (Vision, Viña Montes)	Pride in winemaking.
Airbnb's mission is to create a world where anyone can belong anywhere. (Mission, Airbnb)	Belong anywhere.

Some of the messages contain abstractions. But their references are clear and easy to recognize. This clarity is more pertinent when the message is strategic. And even more so in the case of a strategic corporate definition, such as purpose, mission, or vision. You can see the difference between strategic definitions and their slogans. Viña Montes' vision and Airbnb's mission have a clear reference. But in their respective slogans "Pride in winemaking" or "Belong anywhere" it is vaguer. Visualizing is also more challenging (See Tables 38 and 39.)

TABLE 39

STATEMENTS
(1)   Laws are an invention of the weak to control the strong (Callicles, 484 B.C.).
(2)   You must love your neighbor as yourself (Matthew 22:39, 70-90 A.D.).
(3)   News is what somebody does, not want you to print (Anonymous).
(4)   Social progress can be measured by the social position of the female (Karl Marx, 1848).
(5)   Airbnb's mission is to create a world where anyone can belong anywhere. (Airbnb, 2022).
(6)   The most important single fact about free market is that no exchange takes place unless both parties benefit. (Milton Friedman, 1981).

REFERENCE			
Subject / Agent	**Verb / Action**	**Object / Complement**	**Mode (how) / End (for what)**
Laws	Are	Invention of the weak	To control the strong
You	Must	Love your neighbor	As yourself
News	Is	What somebody does not want you to print.	
Social progress	Can be measured by	The social position of the female.	
Airbnb's mission	Is to create	A world	where anyone can belong anywhere.
Most crucial free market's fact…	Is that	No exchange takes place	Unless both parties benefit

Slogans sacrifice referentiality—not because they miss their target. They do it on purpose.

It is part of a technical resource that stirs the audience's emotions. The technique has been used in applied logic, literature, and the arts.

In logic, arguments are a complete coherent unit. Aristotle called these kinds of arguments *dialectical syllogisms.*

However, in rhetoric, reasoning is better if some premises or conclusions are left out. Sometimes because they are obvious, and others because they are implicit.

This truncated *rhetorical syllogism* received the name of *enthymeme.* In logic and rhetoric, it does not seek explicitness like the dialectical. On the contrary, it uses concealment.

Because that prompts the audience to fill the gap with their amalgam of prejudice and opinions.

We can see how slogans lose rhetorical strength the more explicit they become (see Table 40.)

TABLE 40

Our pride in winemaking is the competitive advantage that sets us apart	more explicit and referential	Our mission is to offer a travel experience where anyone can belong anywhere
We are a pride in winemaking company	(+)	A world where anyone can belong anywhere
A pride in winemaking company		Where anyone can belong anywhere
Pride in winemaking defines us	(-)	We help you to belong anywhere
We take pride in winemaking	less explicit	We belong anywhere
Pride in winemaking	& referential	Belong anywhere

Many of the most revealing and persuasive phrases come from art. From literature, poetry, theatre, and cinema. Many of them use concealment and spin their messages in the same way as slogans or enthymemes. They use rhetorical figures, such as metaphors, comparisons, and hyperbole. They also resort to showing instead of telling through scenes and images. The following example is an excerpt from Homer's *Iliad*, one of the oldest analogies in Western literary tradition.

Very like leaves are the generations of men.
Now the wind scatters the old leaves across the
earth, now the living timber bursts with the
new buds and spring comes round again...
one generation flowers, another dies away.
HOMER, THE ILIAD

The analogy compares two clear images. One is of birth, the other of death — the wind scattering old leaves and the burst of new buds on the timber.

Then, 2,600 years later, in 1913, American poet Ezra Pound followed Homer's path in his celebrated poem *In a Station of the Metro.*

The apparition of these faces in the crowd:
Petals on a wet, black bough.

EZRA POUND, IN A STATION OF THE METRO.

Here, Pound covers the same subject using an analogy containing two images. Inspired by Japanese Haikus, he wanted to produce vivid depictions using precise language.

In just 20 words, he juxtaposes the images of a crowded subway station and petals on a tree branch. With that, Pound relates what the speaker sees ("faces in the crowd") and what he imagines in response ("petals on a wet, black bough.")

To make the association raw and spontaneous, Pound goes further. He adds rhetorical concealment and strips the poem of any explanatory word. He even took off all the verbs (see Table 41.)

TABLE 41

Seeing all these people's faces pass by in a crowded subway station recalls the image of…	
The apparition of ~~people's~~ faces in the crowd of a metro station looks like	Petals on
The apparition of these faces in the crowd ~~of a metro station~~ is like	a wet, black
The apparition of these faces in the crowd are ~~like~~	bough
The apparition of these faces in the crowd	

Poetry takes its epistemological function seriously, though. Traditionally, as a bard, the poet gives us access to the world's truth. They help us discover it. A truth better described by the Ancient Greek word *aletheia.* It is the unveiling of the actual self, not the objective-logical truth expressed by the Latin term *veritas.*

This vocation of disclosure is also found in poetry's avant-garde and fringes. You can find it even in Nicanor Parra's anti-poetry or Charles Bukowski's free verse. It's art as cultural expression. One that operates in the same sphere of religion and philosophy. According to Hegel, this is the central and defining feature of a work of art. The fact that "through the medium of sensation, it presents the most fundamental values of its civilization."[63]

If we look at Homer's passage, the main referents are man's life and the leaves of trees. The meaning, on the first level, is a simile or comparison. But the allusion to being swept away by the wind and the blossoming bud tells us about fragility. In existential terms, it turns into futility. This completes the meaning of the comparison: the lives of men are as futile as the leaves of trees.

Pound's poem tells us something similar. But the sudden appearance of "these" faces from the crowd as petals on a wet, black bough evokes something else. It recognizes personal humanity among the opaque, alienated masses of modern urban life.

Still, both poets deal with the same theme. It is called *ubi sunt,* which means "Where are they?" The phrase was taken from the Latin rhetorical expression, *Ubi sunt qui ante nos fuerunt,* meaning "Where are those who were before us?"

In the Iliad passage, this truth emerges from facing our smallness in the face of nature. In Pound's poem, though, nature is obscured by the meaninglessness of modern life.

---

63 Stanford Encyclopaedia of Philosophy, 2018.

People have recognized the sour truth of *ubi sunt* as a literary topic since the Middle Ages. It can be found in classics by authors like Virgil, Ovid, Boethius, and Shakespeare. It's also in Romantic poets like Shelley, whose poem *Ozymandias* is referenced in the 2017 film *Alien: Covenant.* Contemporary writers such as Edgar Lee Masters, Joseph Heller, and Martin Amis also address the topic. And so do musicians such as Don McLean, Paul Simon and David Bowie.

Advertising can also deliver brilliant, revealing insights. Most of them are delivered when campaigning for humanitarian or social causes. Some of those insights convey universal truths. However, their proneness to simplification breeds an undertone that sounds phony. It did not sound as bad before, in the eighties or nineties. But today, that tone echoes in the resonance box of a different context—a new scenario characterized by the exhaustion of mass media and marketing's traditional rhetoric.

Advertising has made efforts to overcome its superficiality. But in that quest, it has privileged irony. This was a cultural trend that writer David Foster Wallace recognized in American television and literature of the late eighties and early nineties.

In his notable 1993 essay, *E unibus Pluram: Television and US Fiction,*[64] Foster Wallace showed how irony's negative nature serves well to post-modern capitalism. Irony is, above all, a tool to de-sacralize, de-solemnize, de-sublimize and de-construct. Its first celebrated exponent, Socrates, uses it in Plato's early dialogues to the hilt in a crusade to demolish conventional knowledge. Hence, those dialogues received the name *aporetic*, from *aporein*, which means "to doubt." It left a media landscape, argues Foster Wallace, where people wonder whether anything is worth valuing.

---

[64] Foster Wallace, D., 1993.

But all this, in the end, backlashes to advertising. It reinforces the suspicion against the media on the part of the audience. Besides, there is always a looming danger of undermining clarity due to slogans' natural loose referentiality. This makes using them as messages a bad idea. You should never dispense a message in favor of a slogan unless you are sure the reference and meaning are sound and clear beforehand.

Still, you are putting yourself at an unnecessary risk. Better leave that to the poets and artists. Slogans, taglines, catchphrases, and likes to have a persuasive function before a cognitive one. That's why they work much better *with* the message, whether preceding or following, as a compliment.

Indeed, this has become one of the usual ways *The Economist* presents its articles to its readers. A catchphrase or "sloganish" neologism or concept goes first. Then comes the explanatory, referential description. It's also how publishers often title non-fiction books—especially the ones with a vocation of intelligent best-sellers. You can see this tandem in the following examples (see Table 42.)

Some of them have already been mentioned or referenced in this book.

TABLE 42

TITLE (CATCHPHRASE)	MESSAGE
Men Adrift:	Badly educated men in rich countries have not adapted well to trade, tech (…)
Clownfall:	Britain After Boris.
Enough Said:	What's Gone Wrong with the Language of Politics.
Made to Stick:	Why some ideas survive, and others die
Antifragile:	Things that Gain from Disorder
Globalization's Offspring:	How the New Multinationals Are Remaking the Old.
The Vertigo Years:	Europe, 1900-1914.
Words that Get Results:	A Practical Guide to Strategic Messaging

5.2. The order of the factors does alter the product

There are also more practical principles here. The audience can be hostile, skeptical, neutral, or favorable to the message or subject. The speaker's ethos can be low, regular, neutral, or high.

These are four options each, which together form 16 possible combinations (see Table 43.)

Only when you are sure that the audience likes the issue and that you are credible can the message go first.

The messages convey meaning broadly, not just the specifics of the evidence. So, we call this order deductive.

In all the other cases, you should choose an inductive execution: evidence first, message later (supported by the evidence.) An audience may see a message as hostile or dubious.

This can easily trigger an emotional response. The response messes up the message's processing. Although that interference is temporary, it is usually long enough to block or distort the audience's thinking or use of the evidence.

Likewise, the audience may be very favorable to your message. But they will only buy the message if you have enough credibility. All this makes deductive messaging like marriage.

You need to have high credibility and a favorable disposition for a deductive approach. Similarly, you need both spouses' will to continue together. Miss one, and it's over.

As with divorce, which requires only the will of one of the spouses, the odds favor inductive messaging.

TABLE 43:

		AUDIENCE'S STAND ON THE ISSUE			
		Favorable	Neutral	Skeptical	Hostile
SPEAKERS' CREDIBILITY (ETHOS)	High	*Deductive*	*Deductive*	Inductive	Inductive
	Neutral	*Deductive*	Inductive	Inductive	Inductive
	Regular	Inductive	Inductive	Inductive	Inductive
	Low	Inductive	Inductive	Inductive	Inductive

Of the 16 resulting possibilities (see Table 43,) only 3 (20%) should be deductive messaging in comparison to 12 (80%) that correspond to be inductive. So, structuring the messaging is predominantly inductive. However, building a strategic message is always a deductive process. There is an 80% chance that you need to revert the order. This is why this step is so important. Most of the time, you will have to inverse the order of the speech for its execution (see Table 44.)

These principles have nothing to do with nonverbal communication yet. They are about the most suitable order of the speech when executed. They provide a framework of strategic rules. These rules apply directly to the structure of the script, to its logic and logos.

TABLE 44

MESSAGING PROCESSES	
I. BUILDING, PREPARING	**II. EXECUTING, PERFORMING**
1. Build the message using the SMM© equation	4. Present credentials that reinforce your ethos
2. Provide supporting evidence	5. Show the message's supporting evidence
3. Calibrate according to ethos and evidence.	6. Deliver the message

EXAMPLE		
MESSAGING SPEECH	➡	**EXECUTION SCRIPT**
1. Criticizing the dam will make you popular with young people [message]	[ethos]	1. We (Patagonia) have credibility among young people
2. 90% of young people oppose the dam project. [evidence]	[evidence]	2. 90% of young people oppose the dam project.
3. We (Patagonia) have credibility among young people [ethos]	[message]	3. Criticizing the dam will make you popular with young people

Shifting the order has another advantage: It helps to maintain the message's clarity. Sometimes, the message can come across as too direct or too assertive. This often happens when audiences are too formal or authoritative. They are prone to political correctness and easily offended. When faced with this, the immediate and natural response is to tone down the message. We mitigate it.

For instance, suppose I have a boss who is only interested in promoting himself to the board of directors. I want him to approve the Delta project, which I would lead. I have evidence that the Board would well receive the project.

So, to get my boss to approve the Delta project, I need to appeal to his interest in showing off in front of the Board. The key message is: "The Delta project will help you show off in front of the Board."

This may sound too assertive for an audience who is my immediate hierarchical superior. But it can be toned down. First, by modifying the verb. "*The Delta project* **could contribute** *to show you off in front of the Board.*" But sometimes, this form of mitigation can harm the message. The verb usually forms the strategic fundamental semantic relation. So, in some cases, mitigating the verb causes the message to become weak, confusing or condescending.

Yet, there is another form of mitigation. It consists of making the key referents of the sentence less particular and more generic. By doing this, you add abstraction to the refere0nce, which makes the message less sharp, without sacrificing the role of the verb (See Table 45.)

TABLE 45

STATEMENTS' REFERENCE			
Subject / Agent	Verb / Action	Object / Complement	Mode (how) / End (for what)
The Delta Project	Would help	Promoting our area	Within the company's directives.
	Will help	You	Showing off in front of the board.

However, any mitigation can undermine clarity. The most important rule here is never to sacrifice clarity. That is why, in all cases, you must always end until the end of the messaging process. This includes, of course, preparing the execution script.

Only when the message is ready to rumble in the execution script (usually at the end) can I evaluate whether to mitigate it. Never before. I even recommend reading the script out loud a couple of times.

See how it sounds and looks. Check if it still sounds overtly direct or assertive. It usually doesn't.

As preceded by credentials and evidence, the message's perception — not the message itself— soothes. This is thanks to the previous inception of rational elements provided by the evidence and credentials. Only if the message still seems or sounds too assertive do we intervene.

KEY TAKEAWAYS OF CHAPTER 3

➢ Truthfulness and credibility are essential for persuasive communication.

➢ Strategic messages are not slogans. Messages should be clear, referential, and truthful, while slogans can be more creative and less explicit.

➢ Referentiality is key. Messages should refer to concrete and objective entities in the world, like scientific writing and storytelling.

➢ Truthfulness and credibility matter. Messages should be plausible and supported by evidence to maintain the speaker's credibility.

➢ The order of the message, evidence, and credentials should be adjusted based on the audience's receptiveness and the speaker's credibility.

➢ The digital age presents challenges and opportunities: The rise of mass self-communication requires messages that can withstand scrutiny and resonate with diverse audiences.

➢ Truthfulness and credibility are essential: Messages should be plausible and aligned with the audience's understanding or supported by strong evidence.

PART II:

THE CASES

CHECK THESE OUT

The following are four real cases. All of them used the SMM© described in this book, which was applied from its strategic conception to its delivery. The four cases are different. In that sense, they are an empirical demonstration of the universality and applicability of the model and its method. They show versatility in adapting to diverse situations and obtaining good results.

The following table displays the four cases. It shows their differences in challenge, channel, industry, and audience, among others. This gives readers a practical experience of the different application possibilities. It also guides their use to the most likely communication challenges they may face (see Table 46.)

TABLE 46

		CASES		
		1. Worried about your future?	2. Raising the price of a bad...	3. It's your legacy, President	4. Helping the feuds
Audience Description (composition)		Prospective High-net-worth clients (profile)	Purchase Manager of Retail company (Individual)	President and Head of State (Individual)	Regional heads (CEOs) of a global full-service bank (group)
Media, channel		Email	Face to face meeting	Written and phone briefing	Videocall presentation
Industry		Insurance	Logistics	Government	Banking
Audience's Area		Sales	Commercial	Direction	Client Relations
Audience's Challenge		Commercial	Pricing	Political	Consulting
Communication's Area		External	External	Internal	Internal
Levers to use (number)		One (n)	One (n)	One (n)	Six (n + 5)
Accom-plishment	Outcome	Yes	Yes	Yes	Yes and no
	(end) Goal	Yes	Yes	No	Yes

CASE 1

WORRIED ABOUT YOUR FUTURE?

W e were helping an insurance sales team.[65] Their main product is a voluntary, tax-free savings account that contributes to the pension fund. The client profile comprises ordinary citizens: young parents, salaried workers, and self-employed workers. But since the country's provisional system delivers low pensions—well below the person's average lifetime salary—almost everyone's sole interest is improving their retirement funds.

However, a corporate merger caused the team to take over a client portfolio. The team added it and moved on with business as usual, using the same approach, actions, and speech as with their other client portfolios. The first point of contact was almost always a cold email sent to the potential client.

A week later, the sales team realized they were doing something wrong. They had yet to receive a response from any high-net-worth clients.

So, we turned to our SMM© method.

---

65 This case happened in Chile, where the provisional system is based on fully-funded individual capitalization run by private asset management companies. This means that a portion of each worker's (independent and salaried) paycheck is added to their personal pension savings account. Therefore, it's in each worker's own interest to see their fund bulk up over the years.

The sales team thought again and planned. They reviewed the key factors. They found that they made a big mistake. Their whole story was based on the need to get a better pension. It was to contribute to a client's more secure, less strained, and uncertain future. However, one of the things a high-net-worth client usually has figured out is their future finances. Referring to that as a persuasive lever had no effect.

Even their pitches (whether judgment or assertion) were posed as rhetorical questions. Have you thought about your future? Are you sure that your retirement will allow you to live well? Did you know that over 70% of pensions fall short of 50% of salary? The response was a big NO. They were not worried, not interested, not one of them. From that endpoint on, the possibility of moving forward was almost impossible.

After analysis and discussion, the team concluded that the high-net-worth client is interested in paying less tax. They had evidence that their structured products helped optimize taxes. So, paying fewer taxes became the audience's key motivation. The outcome's target action is to get the high-net-worth client to agree to a meeting. Thus, the message would result from the following question (See Table 47.)

TABLE 47

SMM© EQUATION		
ELEMENTS	QUESTION	APPLICATION
Audience X: High-net-worth client. Motivation Y: Pay less tax. Outcome: accept the meeting proposal	What do I tell an **audience** X, whose **motivation** is Y, to make them **do** Z?	What do I tell **the high-net worth client** (X), who is interested in **paying less taxes (Y),** to **accept a meeting? (Z)**

FIGURE 17:

After looking at the facts, we craft an assertion that gives good evidence. It says: "75% of our high-net-worth clients cut taxes 5% to 15% after hiring our products." Yet, our ethos was weak, as is the case for anyone behind a sales cold email. To strengthen it in emails like this, people use the common contact as credentials: "Duncan Smith gave me your contact." This suggested a final change to the message. It should sound more analytical and less like marketing (we are talking about paying less tax!).

FIGURE 18:

The audience has an *a priori* favorable disposition on the subject (we are talking about paying less taxes!). Yet, the ethos is weak. Thus, the reasoning must be deductive. Finally, as the communication act was a "cold" email, we applied the style and conventions of email writing (See Table 48.)

TABLE 48

BUILDING PROCESS	EXECUTION SCRIPT / EMAIL
1. The meeting will show you how to pay less tax. 2. "75% of our high-net-worth clients cut taxes between 5 to 15% after hiring our products." 3. Duncan gave me your contact	Dear Malcolm, Duncan Smith gave me your contact, as this may interest you. 75% of our current high-net-worth clients have made tax cuts between 5% to 20% after hiring our products. You can check the details in this <u>report</u>. I'll show you how these tax-saving products work in a 10-minute zoom meeting next Friday morning. Click <u>here</u> to attend. Best regards,

The resulting script was very similar to the execution script shown in Table 48 (see Table 48.) The sales team first adapted the approach to a contact-based one. Then, they started using this script to reach high-net-worth potential clients. After one month, we measured the response rate of their cold emails. It was 11,7%. This was slightly above their 11.2% average response rate. Yet it was much better than zero, where they were before with the high-net-worth segment.

RAISING THE PRICE OF A BAD SERVICE

In October 2021, we counselled Horatio, a commercial manager of one of the country's two most significant transport and logistics companies. Horatio urgently needed to raise the price of the service to one of the three top retail companies in the country. The retail company also had the most significant contract among non-mining clients. For this purpose, Horatio will meet with Dorotea, the retail company's purchasing manager, in two more days.

"The problem," acknowledged Horatio, "is that we have been providing awful service. In fact, in recent months, they have formally complained five times. The service has suffered several interruptions due to the crisis, even leading to stock-outs. And now, on top of it all, I'm coming to raise the price." The situation looked like a gridlock that was difficult to solve.

We scheduled a meeting with Horatio and his two deputies to prepare the speech and the message. The meeting lasted a little over two hours. In it, we followed all the steps of the SMM©. First, we thought, reflected and then planned. We defined the strategic elements of context, ethos, outcome and audience. We found the hinges and built the message using the SMM© equation. Then, we add the audience and calibrate the message according to it and the ethos. Finally, we assembled the execution script and practiced it, having Horatio embody it several times.

Let us move on to the context now. It was the third quarter of 2021. Companies faced the "container crisis" for months. This was due to factory closures in China from COVID-19. The standstill caused supply shortages and reduced global logistics capacity. This led to many containers piling up at top ports worldwide. Shipping one container from China to the U.S. cost USD 4,000 in September 2020. In September 2021, the cost rose to USD 20,000.

All this reduced the container availability of Horatio's company to its historic minimum. At the same time, all its operational costs increased. The two main truck drivers' unions threatened to strike in two days. This is *unless* management agrees to pay their waiting hours (which soared during the crisis) at overtime rates.

As for the ethos, Horatio has been working with the retail company for more than ten years. He has provided them with a comprehensive transportation and logistics service throughout this time. Horatio has taken care of its products from the ports of China to the various distribution centers in Chile, Peru, and Colombia. The service has always been well-valued. As Dorotea entered the company four years ago, she witnessed their good performance before the crisis.

When asked what the objective of the meeting was, the team's original plan was: "to explain why we have provided poor service and to show what we are doing to improve it." As for the audience's motivation, the whole discourse responded to their concern that "service must improve." This was a real and reasonable concern. However, it has the liability of circumscribing the conversation to address service problems. This eroded Horatio's ethos and weakened his bargaining position.

Moreover, the company needed more resources to improve service effectively (it was still amid a crisis.) In the current situation, any promises made along these lines could quickly become impossible to comply with. And that would undermine credibility even more.

So, we started by changing the objective. We turned it into an *outcome* that could work as a semantic hinge. This is an observable action the audience performs during *the same communication act*. After a brief analysis and discussion, we devised "for Dorotea to accept the price adjustment."

The problem was that trying to get her to accept a price increase by alluding to their motivation for improving our service had two flaws. First, it could lead to a potential overpromise. Also, as Dorotea was very sharp, Horatio was sure she would reply, "OK, improve your service first, and then you raise the price." Therefore, we needed to find another (hopefully more strategic) motivation to use as a hinge and leverage.

TABLE 49

		SEMANTIC HINGES			
Conditions to comply		**Outcome's Target action**	**Audience's Key motivation**		**Conditions to comply**
Executed by the audience.	X	For Horatio to explain and justify the poor service.	That the logistics company improve its service.	X	Traction to my outcome
It occurs on the spot.	✓			X	Supported by evidence
It is observable.	✓			✓	Relevant to the audience

Dorotea's retail company has also been facing difficulties. They needed help adapting their processes to the exponential growth of digital commerce. Also, the digital transformation they had been developing was complex, slow, and costly.

Especially problematic for them has been the management and alignment of last-mile transport providers. Not only did their NPS (service quality indicator) drop to its worst figure in history, but the company also began to be publicly recognized as the retailer with the worst delivery experience.

Moreover, all this happened in intense competition between the two large retail companies and international players Amazon, Alibaba, and Mercado Libre.

For these reasons, the audience's motivation we selected for leverage was "the continuity of the transport and logistics service." We thought it would indeed be able to drive them to accept a rate increase. Then, once these strategic elements were constituted and well formulated, the SMM© equation was applied (See Table 50 and Figure 19:)

TABLE 50

	SEMANTIC HINGES		
Conditions to comply	**Outcome's Target action**	**Audience's Key motivation**	**Conditions to comply**
Executed by the audience. ✓	For Dorotea to accept the logistic service's price increase.	For the logistic company to assure the continuity of its service.	✓ Traction to my outcome
It occurs on the spot. ✓			✓ Supported by evidence
It is observable. ✓			✓ Relevant to the audience

We proceeded to build the message through the equation. The audience (X) is Dorotea, and the outcome (Z) is for her *to accept the price increase*. That was relatively straightforward to define. The main challenge was to find the other hinge: the audience's key motivation. But not any, it had to be one that complies with the three technical conditions. First, it had to serve our outcome. Second, the evidence must be available. Third, it had to be relevant to the audience.

We continued our strategic analysis. We realized that the retail company had a lot at stake. Our relationship with them was business-to-business, with big, long-term contracts. Also, our trade involved shipping, transport, and all their logistics. That means dealing with maritime transport, ports, and customs. Also, ocean carriers, tariffs, truck drivers, and unions. Plus, regulations, international law, smuggling, pirates, drugs and other complications of the import-export world.

Only one supplier besides Horatio's company could provide the service that Dorotea needed. Most surely, the service wouldn't be better. They were facing the same difficulties produced by the container crisis. In addition, Horatio's company and its only competitor would always have the BATNA (Best Alternative to a Negotiating Agreement) of going full into mining. In short, Dorotea depends more on Horatio than the other way around.

On the other side of Dorotea's company, the relationship is B2C. It is much more transactional, as retail consumers aren't particularly loyal. Five similar suppliers were available within a click. From my computer or phone. Easy. In that situation, being known as the worst delivery could be disastrous. But if, on top of that, you add escalating stock-outs because my upstream supplier discontinued its service, the situation would turn catastrophic.

So, we decided to go for that. We defined to leverage Dorotea's interest in *ensuring the continuity of our service*. Then, the SMM© equation was executed in the following way. What do I tell Dorotea, who is interested in assuring the continuity of our service, to accept the price adjustment?

This resulted in the following composition of the strategic message. "The price adjustment" [verb] "the continuity of our service" (see Figure 19.)

FIGURE 19:

Then, we calibrate the message according to evidence and ethos. Dorotea trusted Horatio. The previous year of the crisis, they did a good job together. The previous one, too, Horatio had been very helpful to Dorotea, who was new to the job. Also, there was considerable evidence about Horatio's company crisis and its urgent need for more revenues. This will offset the soar costs and assure operational continuity in the face of present contingencies.

Thus, the message can project a reality with a mid-to-high level of probability and certainty. Given the context, we decided to use a strong verb like "ensure" but in conditional form. Also, as high credibility combines with an audience's hostile disposition to the message, the execution script order must be inductive (see Figure 20 and Table 51.)

FIGURE 20:

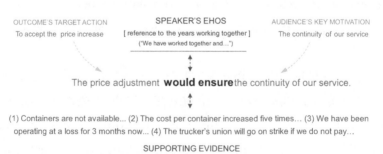

TABLE 51:

		AUDIENCE'S STAND ON THE ISSUE			
		Favorable	Neutral	Skeptical	Hostile
SPEAKERS' CREDIBILITY (ETHOS)	High	*Deductive*	*Deductive*	Inductive	Inductive
	Neutral	*Deductive*	Inductive	Inductive	Inductive
	Regular	Inductive	Inductive	Inductive	Inductive
	Low	Inductive	Inductive	Inductive	Inductive

TABLE 52:

MESSAGING SPEECH		➡		EXECUTION SCRIPT
1. The price increase would ensure the continuity of our service	[message]		[ethos]	1. We have worked together and...
2. "We are in a critical situation" supporting facts and figures.	[evidence]	✕	[evidence]	2. "We are in a critical situation" supporting facts and figures.
3. We have worked together and...	[ethos]		[message]	3. The price adjustment would ensure the continuity of our service

The execution script was then as follows:

1. Hello Dorotea... [greeting-icebreaker]

2. A pleasure to meet you again. Remember when we... [credentials, ethos, small talk]

3. First, I apologize for the latest service shortcomings. We are well aware and concerned. I assigned my deputy, Laertes, to meet with your team to get the details. [objection-response]

4.   Today, however, I come to you with a greater concern. The container crisis has been longer than we expected. It hit us hard... [context]:

5.   Our costs skyrocketed. To give you an idea, shipping one container from China to the U.S. cost USD 4,000 in September 2020. It rose to USD 20,000 in September 2021, a fivefold increase in one year. [evidence 1.]

6.   The crisis also produced logistical mayhem. Today, there is still a 90% deficit in the availability of containers, according to official figures. [evidence 2.]

7.   That mayhem produced new problems that hit you from another front. For instance, Polidoro, the president of the truckers' union, told me last Monday that they would go on strike if we did not pay the waiting hours as overtime. [evidence 3.]

8.   At the beginning of the crisis, we wanted to avoid passing all this cost pressure on to our customers, so we didn't update the rates of our services. We assumed the cost because we thought it would be temporary. But it wasn't, and contingencies kept hitting us.

9.   You are very important as a client, and we trust each other. So, I'll give you an honest picture of our situation, so you have time to prepare. We've been operating at a loss for three months. [evidence 4.] At any time, the board will opt for measures that could put our service on halt.

10. This is why we are asking our clients to meet. I'm hoping that adjusting our rates will be enough to avoid this. In that sense, the price adjustment would help us ensure the continuity of our service [strategic message.]

This script's central theme is no longer Horatio's company's poor service and need for improvement. It's about why a service breakdown is near and how to avoid it. This shift is like what politics calls "changing the narrative."

The original plan was to have this meeting with Horatio to apologize. He would explain, justify, and commit. He would have done so from a weaker position than Dorotea.

Instead, in the new script, it is a courtesy from Horatio. He came to warn Dorotea about the most likely service cut. He also came to request help but clarified that "we" were in the same boat.

Finally, the meeting occurred as agreed. Horatio and his team delivered the strategic message and its speech. They followed the order of the execution script. Then, after a round of questions and answers, Dorotea accepted the price increase.

CASE 3

IT'S YOUR LEGACY, PRESIDENT

This case is particularly magisterial. We will see how the SMM© model applied to a case whose audience was a head of State, a President. It all started when Cassio called us. He was the head of communications at the ministry of environment. We had worked previously together, so he knew the SMM©. Now, Cassio wanted to use it again but on a bigger scale.

The minister of environment at that time was Leontes. He was responsible for a game-changing bill about National Parks and protected areas. The bill moved them from the ministry of agriculture to the ministry of environment. Promising at first, the bill got stuck in the Senate's environment committee. The five senators on the committee had already discussed the bill and amended it. However, an administrative mishap sent it to sleep at the last minute. It had to be woken up and given a little push.

Minister Leontes was a well-known figure in the political world. He had previously held several public positions and had political networks. He knew each of the senators who were making up the committee. So, the strategy was for the minister to approach them individually and have a private conversation with each one. The aim was to get them to commit to the missing step.

Now, why should they do so? Except for one, none of the senators owed minister Leontes a favor or was his buddy. *Quid pro quo* is one of the first rules of the political game. So, minister Leontes needed something to exchange.

We met in a room in the ministry to make a strategic analysis of what the speech would be for the senators. The motivations could be many. Knowing who the person is, and their needs matters a lot in politics. Are they one of us or not? How much of a badass are they? Who's their gang? Who is their 'godfather?' Who 'owns' them? Whose pocket are they in?

After mapping and surveying this individually, we moved to their shared interests. These were three: votes, campaign financing, and media exposure. Nevertheless, the country's situation at the time made the first two dangerous. The system for electing parliamentarians had changed. The outcome of the election changes was still unknown. Votes, therefore, were, for the moment, a fuzzy bargaining chip.

The money used to finance campaigns smelled fishy at the time. This was after several scandals of illegal political financing involving parliamentarians and businesspeople. It was risky.

Media exposure, on the other hand, posed no danger. On the contrary, it was increasingly important to them. We decided on it as a persuasive lever. Minister Leontes would offer the senators high public exposure and media coverage.

Although environmental issues were rising, there had yet to be a milestone that made the front pages and led the national agenda. We needed, thus, to create a milestone that did. Otherwise, it would not be enough to arouse the media hunger of the senators.

After briefly looking at the year's agenda, we saw a landmark. It had the potential to be the hit we needed. An environmental philanthropist and billionaire will donate millions of hectares to the State. The land will be used to create several national parks. It was to be one of the most significant land donations in history.

The donation would also be on land, in the middle of forests and mountains. It was a gift from heaven. But, for it to work, the person who gets the most media coverage had to attend. And that was President Titania. There we had a big problem.

President Titania was at the worst moment in her public history. A month earlier, a scandal had erupted. Her son used his position to make a real estate deal. It was bordering on the legal but quite dirty. The President was slow to react. And when she did, she evaded responsibility. She played dumb. The scandal grew, and she hid.

The result was one of the most significant losses of support in history. From having taken office with almost 80% support, her son's scandal buried her at less than 20%. As it was well known, President Titania lived and worked hard to be loved by the people. That is why the plunge in popularity hit her so hard. She withdrew from the press and stopped attending almost all public events. She limited her public exposure to her daily commute between her home and the government palace.

We could reach the president through minister Leontes. Or through Griselda, her top adviser and close friend. Griselda was also close to Cassio. But how could we get her to attend the donation if she wasn't going anywhere? She was in hiding of her own accord.

We met with Griselda, who confirmed our fears. The president wasn't in the mood to walk around. The only thing she could be available for was something that would earn her the people's affection. "But as you know, that is impossible now," Griselda said. "People just don't like her anymore."

We decided to try anyway. Other times, we had reached a knot and solved it. We had the strategy meeting, and now the audience was

President Titania herself. We were with Griselda. She helped us and tested every draft we were pitching.

Griselda quickly discarded our proposals. We widened our gaze, as we did, for example, in the case of the English wine distributor. In that case, we broadened the scope from price to sales and sales to profits. But here, we found nothing as such. In the end, it all came back to the people's affection.

After hours of trial and error, we found a promising thread. Instead of looking sideways to understand the current context, we had to look ahead. We had to do this as historians. Not as journalists, political analysts, or communication consultants. We must look at how things may evolve in time. We began to prepare the speech. Then, we presented it to Griselda.

It was something like this. "Dear President… people may not support you that much today. But this is nothing compared to the compatriots of tomorrow, the day after tomorrow and so on. Linking your persona with National Parks may tilt history in your favor. It will do so forever. It will make you remembered and loved by all the people who come." Bingo!

So, we apply the SMM© equation (see Figure 21.)

FIGURE 21:

OUTCOME'S TARGET ACTION
President Titania to confirm her
attendance to the land donation act

AUDIENCE'S KEY MOTIVATION
Having a loving, dearing legacy

To **attend to the land donation** + [verb] + **a positive dearing legacy.**
[subject]   [action]   [object]

Then, we calibrate the message according to evidence and ethos. Griselda, her trusted friend and advisor, would be the best option. She said she would do it. Also, there was evidence that national parks catalyzed a president's legacy (see Figure 22.)

FIGURE 22:

OUTCOME'S TARGET ACTION	SPEAKER'S EHOS	AUDIENCE'S KEY MOTIVATION
To confirm her attendance	[reference to Griselda's political instinct] ("You know I've got good instinct...")	Having a loving, dearing legacy

Attending to the land donation **would help to consolidate** a memorable, loving legacy

(1) National Parks are rapidly gaining wide public relevance, media visibility and positive coverage.
(2) Creating National Parks and Protected Areas boosts a president's historical memory and reputation.
(3) Presidents who create National Parks are credited with a positive legacy and are fondly remembered.

SUPPORTING EVIDENCE

However, the link needed to be more direct. It was better to be cautious in what would predicate the verb. Griselda had high credibility, and President Titania favored the message's subject matter.

Yet, it was a "new" issue that needed evidence. It was better to play safe and to go inductive in the execution script.

In this case, evidence mattered big time. The relationship between the issues needs to be reaffirmed. We required the cases and examples to be convincing and fact-based. They also had to strike an emotional chord with President Titania.

As soon as we started on the arguments and their evidence, we realized it was better to use two channels.

First, Griselda would send President Titania a brief with the entire written speech.

Then, Griselda would, either on the phone or in person, reinforce the persuasive effort. She would do this by repeating the speech in her own words.

This was planned to use the virtues of text when presenting facts. The following text was the brief Griselda sent to the President.

1. National Parks are rapidly gaining broad public relevance, media visibility and positive coverage.

   a) Protected areas are essential. Their value is not just environmental but also social and economic. And it can only increase. In 2010, a GEF-WEF-UNDP study estimated that services from protected areas were worth US$1.367 billion annually. Adding priority sites for biodiversity conservation raises this to US$ 2,048 million a year. These include private protected areas. It values ecosystem services, including climate, water, and air regulation (CO_2 capture). They also include erosion control, soil formation, pollination, water cleaning, and pest control. They provide genetic resources, tourism, and food and fiber. A balance has yet to be reached. Globally, humans are encroaching on the ecosystem. Biodiversity loss is increasing. So, the value of protected areas will grow.

   b) Issues of biodiversity protection and protected areas are becoming more critical, and the public values them more. Ten topics went viral globally: in 2015, a North American dentist killed Cecil the lion in Zimbabwe; in 2016, rescuers saved a sloth trying to cross a road in Ecuador; in 2016, over 3 million people visited one of the country's 101 National System of State Protected Wildlife Areas units. This was more than twice the number recorded just a decade ago.

   c) It responds to citizens' current demands, concerns, and values. The results of the citizens' meetings in the Constituent Process show a primary concern for the right to "live in a pollution-free environment." Another problem realized is the scarce provision of public goods. National Parks provide both protected areas and ecosystem services. They are for "the use and enjoyment of all citizens."

d) In the past three years, environmental issues on social media have become more popular. The number of followers of the ministry of environment's Facebook page grew from 30,925 users in April 2014 to 316,000 in January 2017, a tenfold increase.

2. Creating National Parks and Protected Areas boosts a President's historical memory and reputation.

a) It makes a "public" and long-lasting legacy. For example, Murray & Blessing's academic ranking is based on interviews with over 1,000 historians. It and the media rank Theodore Roosevelt as the 5th or 6th best US President. They also rank him as one of the most influential. This is due to his fight against extensive business corruption through antitrust laws. It is also due to his deep commitment to conservation that he has created many national parks.

b) This donation capitalizes on a donation of protected areas that will have historic repercussions. The donation plus the land the state provides will total 4.5 million hectares. This is the largest land national park created in the country in 50 years. They are for the fun and wellbeing of all. This is for today and our children and grandchildren forever.

3. Presidents who create national parks are credited with a positive legacy and are fondly remembered.

a) One of the most emblematic examples is the teddy bear. The name "Teddy bear" comes from Theodore Roosevelt, president of the United States between 1901 and 1909, after he refused to shoot a bear on a promotional hunt. President Roosevelt was often called the 'conservation president' due to his significant impact on the national park system. He signed laws that created five new national parks, doubling their number. Today, the figure of Theodore Roosevelt receives an unspoken homage from families around the world in the teddy bear present in almost every child's bedroom.

Finally, Griselda sent the minutes to the president and met with her after ensuring she had read them. Within a few minutes, she convinced the president (Griselda later told us that, essentially, Teddy had done the magic.)

Ultimately, the President attended the donation in an official act that received enormous media coverage. It made headlines not only in the national but also in international media. Even Hollywood celebrities such as Leonardo DiCaprio dedicated several tweets and posted them on their social networks.

The successful briefing, which effectively mobilized President Titania, was a pivotal moment. Her active role in the donation ceremony was vital to achieving the first part of our strategy. Now, we have a big media event. It backs the idea that Minister Leontes has something real to offer the Senators. This would encourage them to complete the missing step of the bill. It would propel it forward from the senate commission, which was our goal.

Our strategy for the senator's conversation was in full swing when Minister Leontes resigned. He had to leave to lead Senator Hermia's new presidential campaign. As she was his party leader and friend, he was obligated to take on this role.

The problem was that we lost a critical strategic agent. Undersecretary Benvolius assumed the role of minister by default. Despite his strong technical and academic background, he lacked enough political skills. He was also short in political history, networks, or influence. His ethos was insufficient, even detrimental, to engage in that kind of conversation with senators.

We decided to try anyway. We prepared the speech. We trained the secretary. We chose the most accessible and friendly senator to convince. But the meeting was still a disaster, so we gave up on further attempts and discarded the strategy.

CASE 4

CONSULTING THE CONSULTANTS

n this case, we advised Gertrude and her teams. She led a global bank's Customer Relations (CR) division recently formed as a cross-functional unit. Its primary purpose was to improve customer relationships and experience.

The unit consisted of six executive teams plus Gertrude's corporate team. The teams had 2-3 senior executives each and worked at the senior management level.

Each CR team was assigned to one of the bank's six regions. They were Africa and the Middle East, Asia, Europe, Latin America and the Caribbean, the United Kingdom, and the United States and Canada.

After our first meeting with Gertrude's team, we set the goal as "to increase consistency." We also set the goal's measures for accomplishment (see Table 53.)[66] Then, we went to meet with each CR executive team, starting in the United Kingdom.

---

66 A simple, straightforward way to define the measures and metrics of accomplishment (or key results) of a strategic goal is answering questions. What were the main issues? What needs to be addressed? What needs to be achieved?

TABLE 53

| STRATEGIC AIM: | MEASURES OF ACCOMPLISHMENT | |
	AREA	KPIS
Increment consistency	Customer satisfaction	CSAT, NPS, complaints rate, client retention, et al.
	Operational success	Operational costs, No. of workflow processes implemented, et al.
	Deployment of the service model	Implementation; Service: customer journey milestones.

Now, when asked who to address to meet those KPIs (to define the audience), it became clear. The six regional heads were by far the most relevant. Each was the equivalent of a CEO of the world region but under the guidelines of the head office. In this role, the Regional Heads (RHs) must be a mix of a competent feudal lord and exemplary bureaucrat of the corporate politburo of the day.

Gertrude's team has the credentials of a corporate area but no formal incentive or punishment tools. Strictly speaking, then, they operate as consultants. As such, they can be listened to and considered —or only listened to— or neither listened to nor considered. And we, for our part, were consulting the consultants.

When the ethos issue was addressed, the CR team saw that it needed validation. This was because it was new in its structure and role. Also, telling Regional Heads what to do was challenging. They were used to huge autonomy and, also, they were RH because they have done things right.

However, despite these flaws, the CRs have strong leaders in Gertrude's team. Their members are widely recognized for their talent — they were hand-picked as a "dream team."

We reviewed the evidence and analyzed the audience one by one. We found they could be approached from four common motivations. The first (and probably most relevant) was their "key results." Under this name key indicators were grouped, such as client satisfaction, cost, efficiency, and internal employee satisfaction. Another interest was to be recognized as top performer. This meant in a way that it would be visible not only to the bank but also to the high echelons of the industry.

Efficiency was also of strategic importance. The bank's current corporate strategy was defined as "doing more with less." It was consistent to its proposition of pursuing international integration, connectivity, and synergy. The current Global CEO of the bank referred to this as "strategic alignment," so we decided to address it as such. Then we went to a lengthy discussion and analysis of what was possible to get from the RHs. Finally, we defined the outcome as "for the Regional Heads to commit to common definitions and actions that increment consistency."

TABLE 54

SEMANTIC HINGES			
Conditions to comply	Outcome's Target action	Audience's Key motivation	Conditions to comply
Executed by the audience. ✓	For the RH to commit to common definitions and actions.	Client satisfaction (internal too), cost, efficiency, performance.	✓ Traction to my outcome
It occurs on the spot. ✓			✓ Supported by evidence
It is observable. ✓			✓ Relevant to the audience

This is a case where we want to leverage more than one motivation (n+1), so the messaging formula should be applied to the variant we presented in a previous chapter. We applied the messaging SMM© equation to each key motivation of the audience (see Table 55.)

TABLE 55

EQUATION > QUESTION			⇒		RESULT > MESSAGE	
What do I tell [X]	…who want/s [Y]	…to make them do [outcome Z]	=	Comm. outcome's target action	Verb	Audience's key motivation
The Regional Heads (RHs)	Key results: client and employee satisfaction, cost, and efficiency.	Commit common definitions and actions that increase consistency.	=	Increment consistency.	Is	Increasingly tied up to our key results (cost, client satisfaction).
	Be a top performer				will reassert	Ourselves (and teams) as top performers.
	Strategic alignment				will be	A landmark of strategic alignment

The three resulting sentences are strategic messages. But none is made central. Remember, when using more than one motivation, each one constitutes a message.

The audience's motivations are not combined or fused. They go into the structure as arguments of a central message.

That central message must be generic enough to cohesively encompass the arguments. Its role is to coherently provide an overall sense, usually by pointing at obtaining a benefit or avoiding harm.

Sometimes, this can be done simply by verbalizing the communication goal or outcome (see Figure 23.)

FIGURE 23

OUTCOME'S TARGET ACTION
The RHs to **commit definitions and actions for consistency**

AUDIENCES' KEY MOTIVATIONS
Show **strategic alignment**
Be a **top performer**
RH's **key results**

[central message]
We urgently need common and commitments to improve consistency

[because...]

[key message 1] **Our key results** are increasingly tied up to our degree of consistency

[key message 2] **Improve consistency will reassert ourselves and our teams** as **top performers**

[key message 3] **It will be a landmark of alignment** to the bank's current **corporate strategy** and **value proposition** of **"doing more with less"** by pursuing international integration, connectivity and synergy.

This variant of the messaging formula lets us use multiple motivations (n+1) for the same audience. In this case, the audience is the Regional Heads. So, we craft the messages and then add the supporting facts of each.

As this was a presentation, not a pitch, we discussed the possible objections the Regional Heads may have and prepared their responses.

Finally, the audience was moderately skeptical of the message. Some of the RHs were reluctant to accept the proposed change, and some were open. So, it was better to start with the evidence. We used an inductive order for the speech. The final script was as follows:

1. [greeting-icebreaker]
2. [fact of how consistency improved efficiency and client and employee satisfaction]
3. [fact of how inconsistency damaged efficiency and client and employee satisfaction]
4. [therefore:] **Our key results are increasingly tied up to our degree of consistency.**
5. [however], you may ask yourself why we should change if we succeed.
6. [because] We face a new and different scenario [+ supporting facts and data]

7.   [also] **Improving consistency would reassert ourselves and our teams as top performers.**

8.   **We would be addressing a challenge of change that is known for being complex and highly valued by the industry,** like [+ fact]

9.   [besides] **It would be an example of alignment with the bank's current strategy and value proposition.**

10. [Because] **It would be a visible case of "doing more with less" by pursuing international integration, connectivity and synergy.** [+ prospective facts]

11. [on the contrary] **Our consistency gaps can harm us all** [+ fact]

12. Everyone knows that change is hard; it takes time and resources, but **it will be worse if we don't change** [+ fact]

13. [For all these reasons], **We urgently need common definitions and commitments that improve consistency.**

We waited for the Customer Relations (CR) teams to meet with their Regional Heads (RH). Then, we conducted a follow-up. We measured the achievement and impact of the meetings. The results were mostly positive. Four of six RHs agreed on definitions and committed to increasing consistency. This is 66.6%.

Of the remaining two, one was unwilling to be convinced. He said he was already very clear about what to do. As for the other RH (North American region), she never received the strategic messages we made together. The RC team for her region —the dreamy consultants— never told her.

Of course, that was disappointing, yet we saw it coming. North America's CR team never believed in the SMM© model or the script because they never *believed* in *us*. We sensed that in the meeting we had with them in New York.

It was our second work meeting with the CR teams, the first with the UK team in London. We worked perfectly together and were well-received from the start. They liked the SMM© method and used it. So, we were cheerful and confident coming from London to New York.

However, the CR team for North America was unenthusiastic from the start. We noticed an a priori barrier, a pre-conditioning factor that generated interference. In that sense, our confidence blinded us. We didn't realize this was quite a different audience. They have a very different culture about what is foreign, what it means, and how to relate to it. This is even more true if that foreign thing is also "Latino."

Let's start with the first impression. We were introduced as a Chilean company at our first meeting in London. This piqued the interest of the attendees. However, in our New York meeting, the four persons we presented to met this fact silently. With undisguised surprise in their eyes, it seemed as if we were in the wrong meeting room. We should've been showcasing our model on Univision, wearing white linen suits in Miami or in Mexico City with our sombreros.

The bank was also a company whose value proposition was its global and multicultural character. So, it was recognized for being attentive to those issues. It was also dedicated to nurturing and promoting diversity. So why did we feel so evidently out of place?

We went straight to the bar as soon as the meeting was over. We chose one just across the street, in Bryant Park. We had to get rid of the bitter taste we had left behind. With piña coladas and tequila *chupitos,* of course.

We discussed and reflected on our failure to learn from it. After a couple of hours and several drinks, we blamed culture.

Both ways. Us and them. So this reflection may contain some alcohol-inspired associations.

The cultural difference was much more significant than it seemed. The layer of corporate culture also obscures the view. The difference was substantial and probably deep-rooted at national, historical, and idiosyncratic levels. It had to do with what is *foreign*. What does it mean, and how do we relate to it?

The United States was already a continent, so, despite being one country, you get cultural differences that can be as acute as the ones that distinguish a Finish from a Corsican. We just came across a team with all its members from deep inland America. Not from New York, California, Washington, or anywhere with a more multicultural complexion.

The difference with the British could even be traced back to their nation-building processes. The British Empire was maritime, like the Athenians. It built itself from overseas resources. In contrast, America built inwards by colonizing and industrializing its vast landmass.

So, for Britons, anything foreign was a source of danger, of course, but also value. It can be a source of richness, diversity and eccentricity. For Americans, in contrast, anything foreign was, first, suspicious. This was even more true when the foreignness was "Latino." The difference was so ingrained that it has an expression in everyday semantics.

For instance, a British ex-girlfriend sometimes called me, a Chilean, 'you Latin boy.' She also referred to her Italian, French and Brazilian ex-boyfriends as such. In most cases, she wouldn't necessarily mean a bad thing. "Latin" was designated for Latin American and Southern European people. It includes all the nationals from the places where Latin languages were spoken. These include people from Spain, Portugal and Italy (sometimes even France) and also from Argentina, Brazil, Colombia, and other Latin American countries.

For centuries, the English ruling class was strongly influenced by Norman culture. Although its early leaders were descended from Vikings, they were quickly absorbed into Norman culture. That meant the French language, Latin heritage and Catholic faith.

Ironically, Latin's cultural influence over English survived the Protestant and Anglican schisms. It also became a tool and mark of the elite.

The English followed the Roman Republic when the British Empire rose to prominence. Like the Roman *intelligentsia* embraced Greek, the English turned to Latin (which included Greek by default) to organize and make sense of imperial expansion.

The British Empire smoothly integrated words from Classical culture to use the Greek and Latin word systems. They used the words to name, group, and explain the new objects, concepts, and categories of the geographical, scientific, and cultural discoveries.

They were already present in astronomy, biology, chemistry, geometry, and physics. Now, they were used for the new needs of map-making, navigation, mechanics, optics, medicine, botany, anthropology, and archaeology. Latin helped them embrace and make use of the foreign.

This process may have something to do with the outsized influence of Oxbridge education. Until the 1950s, it required Greek and Latin proficiency. This was a mandatory requirement for acceptance.

This cultural Latinization has a lexical expression. In contemporary English, words that refer to material objects, like trees, the sky, grass, and the floor, tend to have a Germanic origin. By contrast, the words for ideas, concepts, or abstract things come almost always from Latin. As for the verbs, there is usually a short Germanic version and an extended Latin one. For example, "do" for "act," "have" for "possess," and so on. [67]

However, for Americans, 'Latino' encompasses diverse cultures and nationalities. To most, it mainly means Mexican heritage and, to a lesser extent, Cuban and Puerto Rican. But its definition isn't primarily linguistic. It's predominantly racial and has positive and negative meanings.

For example, a handsome Argentine friend was into womanizing. He told me he was often lucky in London but rarely in New York. He noticed a change when he said he was Argentinean, which was never a problem in England. So, he passed himself off as Italian.

Influenced by our cultural biases, we thought our New York meeting couldn't be much different from the one in London. The Brits and the Americans were Anglo-Saxon executives. They worked in the same global bank. However, the differences were significant between them and among the Americans themselves. Despite being in New York, none of the US and Canada CRs team members were from there.

In sum, we had a meta-failure. We should have recognized our ethos and followed our own advice. We overestimated our ethos's credibility and understanding of the audience. We should have considered and analyzed it far more deeply and rigorously.

---

67 To better visualize this point, the following paragraph is the previous one we have just passed. In it, I marked all the words of Latin origin in italics and those of Germanic origin (I had thought of Gothic, but I can't read it well). The British *Empire* seamlessly *integrated* words from *Classical culture*, *using* them to *name*, group, and *explain* the new world. These words *proved invaluable* in their *geographical, scientific*, and *cultural discoveries*. They *expanded* the *Greek* and *Latin* word *systems*, *initially used* in many *sciences*, to *include new objects, concepts* and *categories*. These *sciences* spanned *astronomy, biology, chemistry, geometry*, and *physics*. Now, they were *used* to encompass the *new realities* of *map*-making, *navigation, mechanics*, optics, *medicine, botany, anthropology* and *archaeology*, among many *others*.

FINAL THOUGHTS

Thank you for allowing me to share this book with you. If you are here, I assume you didn't find its reading unbearable. As you may have noticed, the SMM© model and method are quite structured. For some people, that can make things difficult at first.

The structure gets bad press when it comes to human traits and relationships. If a dating app asks to describe your personality in one word, no one would use "structured." Even if you are, you probably wouldn't use it. It's just not sexy.

However, structure is paramount in strategic communication. The beauty of the SMM© lies, indeed, in its structured and codified nature. It lets you learn the method as a technique. At first, it's a tool that you can use anytime. Then, it's a skill you can practice, perfect, and develop.

Patterns and structure also help make the model more democratic. Once someone learns the method, anyone can use it. They can leverage its power regardless of background. This levels the playing field, making strategic communication accessible to all.

I also hope that you have already been able to test the SMM© model's practical usefulness in a real challenge. This could be by using either some of its tips and techniques or its whole methodology. If you have not, I encourage you to do so sooner rather than later. Don't miss the chance to put this model to the test in a real-world scenario with strategic importance.

What motivates me most is seeing the concepts in this book translated into action. This is why I've written it, to help people improve their communication and make things easier. After experiencing the benefits, I've wanted to share the tool with everyone.

Improving our communications skills may be a challenging journey in itself. That was the case for me. The SMM© model's origin and method come from my own frustration and failure. For years, I've felt that my ideas lost value when I communicated them. And many of the mistakes and failures I regret could have been avoided or diverted.

Although it took me years, I did close the gap. I did it by learning. It can be done. So, don't worry too much if you feel you have a long way to go. The perceived distance to your goals is shorter than it seems. I'm a slow learner, so it's likely that it will easier for you than it was for me.

This model provides a roadmap that saves you time and effort. Think of it as a detour that can help you avoid steep roads and dead ends. All this is to make your journey faster and more pleasant.

It began with mistakes

Of all my old high school classmates, Andrés Crovetto was the least likely to succeed. We were stunned to learn he was living in Zurich with a high-powered banking job. Most of us thought it was a joke. After all, Andrés was always on the verge of expulsion due to poor academic performance. The reason was simple: he didn't like to study. From a young age, he focused his energy in lobbying and sweet talking. Now, he was doing great in Switzerland.

Andrés has a particular physique: short, skinny, whitish, bulging eyes, big ears. He wasn't particularly handsome. But his gregarious, big personality and sense of humor made him good company. He took nothing serious, least of all himself.

On a Sunday night in 1988, one of Santiago's few TV channels aired the Hollywood movie *Mac and Me*. The main character, Mac, looked a lot like Andrés. The next day at school, a group of us went bullying him. We gathered around him and decided to baptize him, Mac. He didn't say anything and waited for the laughter to die down. Then, dead serious, he came with a name that honored his Italian ancestry, Crovetto. But also, his newly discovered extraterrestrial nature.

I'm not Mac, you stupid earthlings. I'm Crovenus.

From that day forward, he proudly introduced himself as Crovenus to everyone he met.

Once, his name almost got him drafted into the Army. We were standing in a cold, foggy military facility courtyard. There were hundreds of 18-year-olds, side by side, with draft notices. An acceptance letter from a university typically meant an exemption. But there was a formal process. You' had to wait in line after showing up and presenting your papers for an interview.

Back then, Chile was a democracy. However, the country was still transitioning from 17 years of military rule. In those days, with the Army, you never knew what to expect. Our ears, forehead, feet, and hands were freezing. But nobody dared complain. Because the one thing we all knew for sure, was that you never mess with the Army. Ever.

After 30 minutes, an officer instructed us to write our full names on little slips of paper. We held them across our chests as he surveyed us. He stopped abruptly in front of Crovenus. I glanced at his chest. He had written in big capital letters: Andreptune Crovenus Che-Guevarum.

"Looks like we've got a comedian here," the sergeant shouted. "Take him inside."

Back then, in 1993, the dictatorship wasn't a distant memory. This made a situation like this unlikely but still possible. He went inside, as he was told, and the rest of us stood there, outside, worried. After two hours, we saw Crovenus emerge from inside the building. He seemed fine. In fact, he was now sipping a coffee and chatting amiably with the sergeant. I saw the sergeant laughing for the first time. Now in a green scarf, Crovenus drained his cup and handed it to a soldier. He nodded to the soldier and returned to the line.

"What happened?" I asked.

"He's my client now," he said. "I'm going to DJ at his daughter's' 17th birthday party. As DJ Crovenus," he added.

We were all stunned. When, on our way out, I reminded him he still had the officer's scarf, he replied that it was a gift.

What happened that day should have helped us to see that Crovenus had been on to something. But we didn't. Instead, we kept on believing that grades and test scores would predict our destinies. We thought the formal knowledge we were learning inside the classroom was everything.

But now, after thirty years, I've come to believe in the vital need for Crovenus-like skills. In the episode that brought his name to life, we were bullying him hard. However, he used his interpersonal skills to turn it around. It was something that could easily end either in a fight or a humiliating capitulation. He slowed down. He thought about and used his humor to win us over. This made him cooler.

Nearly all our forty classmates applied to university. Fifteen studied engineering. Ten studied business, including Crovenus, at a low-prestige university. Five went to law, and three to medicine. The rest scattered across biology, dentistry, and architecture.

We had to fill out our applications on a typewriter. Every mistake meant rewriting everything. Of course, you could use Liquid Paper to make corrections in minor documents. But not for something as formal as a college application. I still recall having to buy extra paper after more than thirty attempts. It was the last decade of the 20th Century.[68]

Once at university, I studied double degrees. I did one in Hispanic linguistics and literature in the morning. Then, I did another in philosophy in the afternoon. I spent most of my time reading and studying. I made summaries (for myself) and wrote essays. Computers were introduced to all students and made available in large campus rooms. So, in the end, I stayed at the university all day between the library and computer rooms.

Socializing wasn't emphasized in either program. Both degrees prepared you to continue in academia. Also, this was humanities in a third-world country. There were only five departments of linguistics and six of philosophy. So, if there were already few academic positions, there would be even fewer in the humanities. The fight for ensuring a place was fierce. Cutthroat as the Iron Throne and backstabbing as the Borgias' court.

Outside academia, the job prospects in the Chilean market were non-existent. Most of my classmates went on to pursue school-teaching qualifications. Others went into publishing or media, while some, like me, landed in advertising.

Initially, I was thrilled. The agency was amid the city's new business district. It occupied an entire floor in a gleaming all-glass new building. Transparent walls separated offices and meeting rooms. Every workstation

---

68 Almost thirty years later, in 2023, I'm finishing proofreading this book using AI applications. Crovenus has sent me a WhatsApp, allowing me to tell his story. He still lives in Zurich, but he's now married with two kids and works as a bank executive.
The German cooking robot Thermomix was loudly making a Peruvian dish in the kitchen. I picked it from its mobile app, which offered recipes from around the world. Turkish, Thai, Italian, Japanese, Mexican, French, Indian, Vietnamese, Greek, Chinese, or Moroccan. I also had two videoconferences during the day. The first was a consulting meeting with an American client using Teams. The second was a lecture on Zoom to a group of start-up owners sponsored by Endeavour, the global non-profit organization that supports high-impact entrepreneurs. I did all this from a cabin by a lake in Northern Patagonia via Elon Musk's Starlink internet. The electricity for all those devices came from the sun, harnessed using Bluetti's four solar panels and two portable power stations.

boasted a colorful iMac G3, and the two receptionists were stunning. Everyone looked like they'd stepped out of an MTV music video.

However, soon my enthusiasm began to fade. They told me that they had made a mistake and had me registered as an unpaid intern. It took them more than a month to arrange the registration, so I spent my savings on transport fare during my first month.

Then, I was summoned by what must have been the human resources manager with one of the partners. I would earn $400 dollars a month. "Think of it like military service," said the big boss. "You are very lucky," the human resources manager added. "Many don't' even get past the internship here." I thought I was lucky for not having left my current rental room. I could keep living there as a student for $200 dollars a month.

"You have the chance to become a Creative," said the partner. "You can make millions having fun doing commercials, dating models and getting invited to the best parties in town."

This promised land also employed ten more junior "soldiers," all unpaid interns. Our 9-to-9 schedule involved tedious tasks. Internet research, updating databases, fact-checking, and photo editing. A lot of tasks were menial too, such as fetching Starbucks coffee or parking cars. We were also summoned to work on weekends or leave the office after midnight.

After a month, I thought, if this was going to be the real world, I'd better find a way to stay at university forever.

I decided to get expert advice and contacted Obi Wan Cannabis. He was a 50-year-old pot-master and the most perennial PhD student in my former university. I had met him playing soccer on the university courts, where he hung out most of the time.

Obi Wan was always there, organizing soccer championships or playing ping-pong and chess. And of course, running a medicinal marijuana business on the side. We became friends.

"What you need to understand is that the university is a subsidiary system," he told me. "Society subsidizes the university; which subsidizes the humanities; which subsidizes our Literature Department. So, it's natural that we get subsidized as well. That's what scholarships are for."

In fact, six persons lived on the Obi Wan scholarship scheme. Him, his girlfriend, his two children, and his two ex-wives. He was now transitioning from receiving a single father scholarship to a senior student one.

While I was applying to every scholarship I could, I was "promoted" to junior copywriter. The job still consisted of performing junior functions, but it involved meetings. Meetings in a busy work environment where everyone competed to be the coolest. It was there that I became aware of my expressive shortcomings and how dire my communication was.

The moment I spoke, interest was lost. I blamed it on being new, inexperienced, and unversed in company culture and jargon. But over time, I realized the problem was me. It didn't matter if it was with my boss, colleagues, or clients. Insecurity and self-consciousness made me talk too much. I gave too many explanations and hedged. This made me sound even more insecure. It was a vicious cycle that dragged on for months. Even Blinky, the laid-back catfish in the fancy aquarium, turned away when I spoke.

I was so lame that I could even bore a fish.

Since that day, I have been attentive to how people communicate and, on a quest to improve my skills. Soon, I discovered that all wasn't lost. There was hope. You can get, train, and hone communication skills. My quest turned into an obsession.

Of course, some people are natural-born, talented communicators. But many of those who appear to be naturally gifted have taken the time to learn a few things on the side. Some get it from formal training, others through extracurricular education. Others from their upbringing or from their family traditions or practices. Some others acquire these skills by following the example of a role model. A person close enough to learn from and mimic.

As soon as I could afford it, I bought books. I also enrolled in the best communication courses and workshops I could find. I started with critical thinking, debating, and storytelling. Then I went to public speaking, negotiation, effective presentations, and crucial conversations. I also sought out the help of coaches and mentors who became invaluable guides in this journey.

After a year in the agency and just starting my learning journey, I won a scholarship to study a master's in London. Obi-Wan's advice had paid off.

I resigned from the agency and moved to London. I arrived in 2002, when the UK was celebrating the Golden Jubilee of Elizabeth II. By then, London was a hotspot of liberal Western culture.

It had become an open, prosperous, multi-cultural global center amid the War on Terror. After I finished my master's, I took a corporate job in London as a marketing executive. By then, I also started freelancing as a journalist in English and Spanish. I wrote on international politics and economics.

Then, in 2008, I returned to Chile to work as a communications advisor for the minister of the interior. The minister named me his lead speechwriter and in charge of the government's narrative. From the other side of the world, I saw how the Subprime Crisis ended up being a pivotal event. Francis Fukuyama said it represented the end of Reaganism in finance. But it also seemed more than that. German historian Philip Bloom said it marked the end of neoliberalism's legitimacy. This is neoliberalism as a fair and beneficial economic model. [69]

---

69 Fukuyama, 2008; Bloom, 2021.

By then, I had been lucky to work in copywriting, marketing, speechwriting, editing, and journalism. After that I have been a consultant, director, and CEO. My work track record has allowed me to visit different parts of the world. Some of these were places I would not have known otherwise. They include Santiago, London, Barcelona, Tunbridge Wells, Washington D.C., and Oslo. I have also been in Mexico City, São Paulo, New York, Buenos Aires, Lima, and Salzburg in a professional capacity.

I met and worked with people from many cultures and countries. Of course, each of them with their own way of seeing and doing things. Yet, all those who were good communicators had two things in common.

The first quality that stood out was emotional control. They were good at staying calm. This was especially true in tense and hard situations. It was a quiet, nonverbal composure. A corporate version of Hemingway's "grace under pressure."

The second essential trait was undeniably verbal: the sheer clarity of their messages. They were articulate people who made communication seem easy and effortless. However, as simple as it looked, such an ability was not a common thing to have.

First, you need to be literate and knowledgeable. However, just possessing a sound amount of knowledge and a rich conceptual world wasn't enough. This is why some academics, researchers, and scientists can come across as dull. Knowledge and vocabulary are crucial, but true communication mastery lies in articulation. It's the ability to express yourself precisely and clearly. It's about ensuring your message resonates with the listener.

These two qualities, emotional control and articulation, work great in synergy. Their combination produces a natural assertiveness that is ideal for leadership. It fosters teamwork, collaboration, influence, and persuasion, all flowing from it. But more importantly, it also keeps aggressiveness at bay, preventing unnecessary conflict.

Behavioral science has shown that humans resort to aggression when lacking communication skills. It usually takes the form of sarcasm, irony, or fallacies like the *ad hominem* attack. Although less often, the aggression can become physical. When overwhelmed by anger or frustration, these people use violence to express their discontent.

Having examined good communicators, I began to recognize similar patterns in their speech. These patterns weren't only about language but also about strategy. They had links to their actions, forming a cohesive whole. As I dug into persuasive communication, I focused on integrating patterns into models. That process of consolidation led me to develop a comprehensive model and method.

What cannot be measured does not exist

For most of the world, the last four decades have been of tech and economic change. But for Chile, the change involved deep economic, political, and cultural shifts. The country went from a poor, isolated, and dictatorship-ridden system to a middle-income democracy with an open society. It is now fully integrated into the world markets.[70] This change ended up creating a market for communications business endeavors like ours.

The heart of Chile's transformation was an accelerated capitalist modernization. It was based on by-the-book free-market principles. This approach came from the rule of General Pinochet. He was a military dictator

---

70 Chile is recognised as one of the exemplary countries that, in the 20th century, was able to move from underdevelopment, poverty, and dictatorship to middle-income and democracy. According to official data from the World Bank, Chile ten-folded its economy in thirty years, from a GDP of 26,04 billion dollars in 1988 to 295,40 billion dollars in 2018. In the same period, the country's GDP per capita grew by a factor of eight, from 2,016 dollars to 15,796. As for poverty, 67% of Chile's population lived under the poverty line in 1987, which was reduced to 7,6% by 2022, almost to one-ninth in less than thirty years.

who seized power in a 1973 coup and held onto it until 1989. Under Pinochet, a group of young economists, called the "Chicago Boys," ran the Chilean economy. They earned their name because most of them got their Ph.Ds. in Economics at the University of Chicago. Their mentors were professors Milton Friedman, Arnold Harberger, and Friedrich Von Hayek.[71]

The Chicago Boys implemented a new economic program. It included widespread liberalization, deregulation, and privatization of state-owned companies and public services. That was radical and unprecedented in the mid 1970s. It hadn't been done yet.

It also involved a drastic 50% cut in public spending. This cut was a brutal "shock treatment" for the Chilean economy. The initial effects were severe. GDP plummeted by 13% while unemployment soared to almost 30%.

After the initial shock, the economy eventually rebounded in spectacular fashion. The Chicago Boys started getting international attention and praise. They were beating inflation, growing exports, and attracting foreign investment. Economist Alan Walters, advisor to Margaret Thatcher and Friedman's friend recalled. "It was fascinating. The great experiment in free market economics."[72] Walters often visited to Santiago to meet with Pinochet and the Chicago Boys. He later became the architect of Thatcherism's economic policies.

The Chicago Boys' economic program was the "first experiment in making a neoliberal state." But, more importantly, it was a blueprint. Chile was a testing ground. It provided a template for doing similar neoliberal reforms elsewhere.[73] In 1982, Newsweek magazine interviewed Milton Friedman, Neoliberalism's Yoda master. He described what happened in Chile as an "economic miracle."

71 Moreno, 2006.
72 Beckett, 2003.
73 Harvey, 2002.

During the 1980s, Margaret Thatcher and Ronald Reagan adopted similar economic policies. This unleashed a global wave of policy mirroring the Chicago Boys' model. The 1989 Fall of the Berlin Wall and the end of the Soviet Union weakened collectivist economics. Fukuyama's End of History was coming. With it, came the Chicago-boys' style neoliberalism, which became the economic orthodoxy.

Ironically, in Chile the same year of the Berlin Wall fall, 1989, democracy was restored. A coalition of center-left parties defeated Pinochet and began rebuilding democratic institutions. However, the center-left governments held on to the Chicago Boys' monetarist model. Instead of using socialist economic policies, they chose to keep their predecessors'.

Chile's apparent success buoyed Friedman. Business schools, corporate boards, and senior management treated his theories as gospel. They also adopted his staunchly economic-focused world view. A rational, quantifiable market was the best way to regulate all parts of life. It was also fairer. Every reality could –and should– be reduced to numbers. The Chilean business community of the time echoed a common mantra: "If you can't measure it, it doesn't exist."

It was then that I became aware of something I would later confirm. Spreadsheets are fantastic tools. Numbers and Excel are great at optimizing existing realities. They streamline organizations, sharpen business models, and inject dynamism. However, their power lies in refinement, not revolution. They're ill-suited for creating entirely new things. To borrow from Aristotle, Excel thrives with kinetic changes – tweaks and adjustments. But for metabolic changes, which fundamentally transform something, words are the key.[74]

---

74 In his book *Physics*, Aristotle distinguishes two kinds of changes affecting all natural beings. On the one hand, there is accidental change or motion (*kinesis*), and on the other, substantial change (*metabolè*), which is when a change of being occurs.

At that time, Chilean society ––and by extension, its businesses—had faced a difficulty. It was the lack of transformative language. The country had endured a brutal 17-year dictatorship. After it ended, there was a long cultural blackout. The military regime had closed university departments such as sociology, politics, anthropology, and most humanities. It had clamped down on the media. It handed control to right-wing business leaders with very conservative agendas. The blackout was imposed and sustained by a military with the cultural finesse of a hot dog. The market of ideas shrank to a minimum.

The blender was filled with a strange mix. It had military machismo, a strong dose of neoliberalism, and a twist of 80s glam. This was in a country where its people have never been particularly known for being stylish or entertaining.[75] The result was a moronic sublimation. It brought the traditional dull and ungraceful character of the country to new heights of moronism. This was especially true for men.

I remember one occasion in my first or second year of university. I was at my friend's birthday party barbecue. Him and his friends had attended one of the most exclusive high schools in the country, so when I said I was studying linguistics and literature, a guy asked, disgusted, WHY?! He was wearing a pale blue shirt, khaki dockers and trekking sneakers.

---

75 Fashion can summarize the spirit of its time, or at least eloquently express it. Those years saw the birth of one of the most representative outfits of the successful Chilean man. So much so that to this day, it is practically a uniform among executives or wannabees. The attire consists of a Ralph Lauren or Lacoste pale blue shirt, khaki dockers trousers and… Columbia or Merrell trekking shoes (!). In 2022, Imagen Chile conducted a study asking people around the world what is the first word that comes to mind when they think of the country Chile. The cities chosen were 12 capitals: Sao Paulo, Toronto, New York, Washington, London, Berlin, Paris, Madrid, Shanghai, Tokyo, New Delhi and Dubai. The study found that, after a generality such as "South America", which ranked first, the second most common thing that came to mind was "Nothing." This is consistent with the fact that most South American countries are larger and more populated than Chile, with warmer climates, livelier cultures and slimmer, better-looking people who are better at football, sports, modelling, and dancing.

"Because I like to read," I replied.

"Me," he puffed out his chest "I don't read. I rather watch the movie."

This kind of "popular wisdom" and cultural contempt was usual in the Chilean elite. Conversations needed nuance and critical thought. But the replies were painfully basic or leaned on conservative-neoliberal machismo. Like in Communism or Fascism, language was used to reduce or simplify reality. This context fostered a shallow, stifled language. It could not compete with the pumped-up reality of numbers. Words, it seemed, were irrelevant. They didn't matter.

That was the backdrop against which we had to sell soft skills and communication. Messaging and storytelling were like palmistry or astrology for the business community. Caring about writing went beyond basic grammar and spelling. It was seen as "artistic," a synonym for ornamental and a euphemism for a waste of time. It was far more productive —and persuasive— to speak with numbers.

To break into the market, my team and I concentrated on two things. First, our solutions had to be unequivocally objective. Communication was still an airy idea for our potential clients. They were mostly conservative business owners, CEOs, and top managers. So, we knew that most of our first meetings would be acid tests. This was even more reason to double our efforts in integrating and codifying patterns to structure models. We needed to propose something solid and elegant. It would resist a blow from Grandmaster Yoda-Friedman himself. He wore a pale blue shirt, khaki dockers, and trekking shoes.

The second critical element was that our solutions had to be versatile. Exports and domestic consumption surged. This fueled rapid diversification and liberalization in the Chilean market. Democracy sped this up. So did the ongoing digital and Internet revolutions. From 1993 to 2022, the nation's total exports grew ninefold.

They rose from USD 12.76 billion (25.8% of GDP) to USD 107.38 billion (35.67% of GDP).

One prime example of this transformation is the Chilean wine industry. Export-focused modernization began in the late 1980s under military rule. But it was under democracy that the industry truly flourished. In 1988, before Pinochet left, Chile shipped only 185,630 hectoliters of wine abroad. By 2022, it had exploded to 8.33 million hectoliters. That's a 45-fold increase in just 35 years.

Growth was similar on the domestic front. In 1990, there were fewer than 100 wineries. Today, there are over 800 active wineries and 11,697 producers. There are also 394 export companies. They are mostly small and medium-sized enterprises (SMEs). They all contribute to Chile's vibrant wine scene.[76]

The increases made Chile the world's' fourth-largest wine exporter. It trails only France, Italy, and Spain. It's also the leader in the Southern Hemisphere and among New World wine producers.

Today, the country holds the title of top exporter. And it's not just wine, but also of copper, salmon, and high-value fruits and berries.[77]

These changes happened at the same time as a 25% population growth. The population grew from 14 million in 1989 to 19 million in 2022. The percentage of immigrants also rose from 1.2% in 1989 to almost 9% in 2022. In broad terms, this means growth by addition but also by transformation.

Our first clients were multinationals entering the Latin American market through Chile. Or domestic companies expanding to other

---

76 Wines of Chile, 2024.
77 It is the first exporter of copper, grapes, fresh cherries, prunes, and dried apples; the second-largest exporter of salmon fillets, fresh plums, shelled walnuts, shelled hazelnuts, raspberries, blackberries, and frozen blackberries.

countries. In either case, they needed to address segmented domestic and foreign audiences.

By then, it was clear that Excel spreadsheets were not enough. The new era had complex economics and society. Companies needed a metabolic transformation, not just a kinetic one. Here, the impoverished language of a culturally stifled Chile fell short. This created fertile ground for communication products, including those we offered.

When strategically used, language serves as a powerful tool. It helps transform cultural capital into conceptual one. Concepts are the building blocks we use to organize and make sense of reality. They become especially crucial as our world grows ever more complex. Through concepts, we see patterns. They help us plan and, in the end, predict the future.

This was even more reason for our models to embrace complexity. We needed tools that could work well in diverse industries, sectors, and situations. They also had to work across national cultures. In other words, we had to be agile and adaptable. So, we made this reality dynamic and diverse. It's always shifting. And we made it a basic part of our system.

We discovered that addressing diverse audiences with segmentation took a lot of work. It led to an expanding kaleidoscopic atomization. It became clear that working in the opposite direction would be more efficient. We needed a single, cohesive model. It could address this variety for everyone. We didn't need many versions. That meant Universal, with a capital U.

To achieve this universality, the model had to fit both nature and function. It needed to be based in fields that go beyond cultures and societies. These were disciplines with principals that went beyond fleeting trends and fashions. They worked across the boundaries of space and time.

In his book *Antifragile*, essayist and mathematical statistician Nassim Taleb presents a dichotomy. The probability of survival among living beings, including humans, decreases with time. The older we get, the closer we are to obsolescence and death. Each day in this fleeting life makes life shorter. Unlike the expiration dates of technologies, disciplines, and ideas which increase with time. "For the non-perishable," says Taleb, "every day implies a longer life expectancy."[78]

For example, a technology like the wheel dates back 6,000 years. That makes its life expectancy much higher than that of the Blue Ray, which has been around for only a decade. Likewise, a work such as Plato's *Republic* is 2,500 years old. This gives it a much higher probability of staying "alive" for the next 1,000 years than *Fifty Shades of Grey*. Time favors the relevant while wiping out what can be hype or noise.

In that way, vocational subjects, like computer programming, may be riskier. Someone who studied how to punch IBM cards has a tiny job market today, if any. In the 1980s, learning Japanese was popular. After all, its cars and electronics were conquering the world. Fast forward to today. The market only remains in specialized scientific and technical niches.

Some disciplines, on the other hand, resist time. These fields have long-standing traditions. They include logic, grammar, arithmetic, and rhetoric. Or, they may be inherent to the very essence of human experience, like storytelling. These disciplines have been with us for thousands of years. This gives them a high chance of staying relevant. The format, medium, institutions, and ideological frameworks surrounding interpersonal relationships may change. Yet, the core need for communication and language itself will remain. We will still need language to name, describe, and explain. It's also for convincing, asking, ordering, denying, threatening, promising, inspiring, and mobilizing.[79]

Today, we are at a historical crossroads. Artificial intelligence is rising. This is happening now. Also, there are never-before-seen advances in gene

---

78 Taleb, 2012.
79 Thompson, 2017.

editing and robotics. This confluence marks the start of what some call the Fourth Industrial Revolution. AI is already reaching into fields like neurobiology, immunology, synthetic chemistry, and nanotechnology. Soon, it will also influence materials science, quantum computing, and particle physics. We haven't even glimpsed the faintest outline. We don't know what will come from their combined actions and synergies. Some experts believe it will affect our lives more than the Internet did. It will affect them more than Gutenberg's Printing Press did.

But, where we are now, one area has proven hard to automate. It's the skills for social and emotional interaction. Machines are great at following rules and doing tasks well. But human interaction is a messy and complex dance. It involves understanding unspoken cues. You must navigate emotional nuances and adapt to ever-changing social dynamics. These subtleties are difficult for current AI to replicate. At least for now.

Great messaging comes with great responsibility

I shared the SMM© model with you in this book. It has brought me work and personal joy. It has given me many great moments. Most were in sterile offices and grand meeting rooms. Yet, I particularly remember two that occurred outside of the business environment. One took place in the bustling aisles of a supermarket. The year was 2012. By that time, I had already embarked on training and coaching managers.

One day, I was buying groceries on my way from work to home. Suddenly, a middle-aged man approached me with a broad smile. I recognized him as Oberon, a manager I had once trained. After effusively greeting me, he launched into his story. He told me he had convinced his boss to let him work from home thanks to the messaging model he learnt from us.

His wife was ill, and he was eager to be close by and available for her. So, he was pleased, to say the least.

Over the years, more people like him have told me how they've used these messaging techniques. Most said it helped them get what they wanted. Even the ones who didn't get what they wanted were always enthusiastic. They talked about recasting their strategy and giving it another try. I am very grateful to them. After all, my aim is to give you the tools. This is indeed the core purpose of this book: provide with tools that will help you navigate life's challenges.

There is, of course, the flip side of the coin. The SMM© model could be misused for selfish, dishonest, or even Machiavellian purposes. People bring up this worry in workshops or facilitations. It often comes as a question or objection. Yet, while the question is entirely valid, the objection is not so much. SMM© can undoubtedly be wielded as a tool for manipulation. However, manipulation is not inherent to its nature. You can effectively use it without resorting to deception or disguise.

The ancient Greeks' term "techne" was a rich concept. It referred not only to the products of technology and technique but also to the fruits of arts and crafts. The word also encompassed the body of knowledge used to produce them. This knowledge ranged from math and music to shoemaking and running a household.

For some, such as Plato, some techniques were inherently more negative than positive. This would be true for rhetoric and poetry. They are different from dialectics and philosophy.

For others, such as Aristotle, *techne* was usually morally neutral. Their goodness or badness depended mostly on how they were used. This is true for the simplest tools our ancestors made from sticks, stones, and bones. It is true for tools all the way up to the Large Hadron Collider. Some creations, like the atomic bomb, the guillotine, or Reggaeton, are inherently bad.

However, I believe this is not the case with SMM©.

The tool itself is not the problem. The ethical issues lie outside it. The user's moral compass and sense of responsibility become clearer and more important. As Uncle Ben wisely reminded Spider-Man, "Great power brings great responsibility." So, it's up to you. The choice is on your side. You can leverage the strategic messaging method to favor truth, not oppose it. You can use it to check liars and manipulators, not aid them. You can keep demagogues at bay instead of surrendering to their views and ideas.

One simple way to avoid the many roads to the dark side is to stay close to the evidence. To have a hold on it and never go beyond —to keep it real. You may encounter Palpatine, Sauron, and Hannibal Lecter types. This is especially true in politics and business. But as long as you remain tethered to facts and truth, you will be safe.

Another instance, much like the encounter with Oberon in the supermarket. This time, however, the setting was far from an office. It was in the middle of the Atacama Desert while I was on vacation with my family and friends.

The Atacama Desert is the driest place on Earth and one of its most sparsely populated regions. It is a high plateau formed by mineral rocks and salt. They have different shapes and colors, as if geological time had engraved it. It is a place full of solitude and silence that also has the virtue of offering the clearest skies of the world.

In 2016, Imagen Chile, the agency that promotes the country's brand, invited my firm to bid. They wanted a narrative about Chile's unique astronomy and sky observation. We won, chose the team, and started working.

Chile was a powerhouse in astronomy infrastructure, investment, and development. But its image abroad didn't reflect that. Astronomy and stargazing were missing from their communication strategies. When mentioned, inconsistent messaging diluted their potential as branding attributes. [80]

After extensive data analysis and stakeholder validation, we crafted a fact-driven narrative. We incorporated it into the brand's strategy and handed it to Imagen Chile. They did an excellent job. Soon, our messages resonated with other stakeholders. These included government ministries, tourism groups, schools, and the media.

Three years later, a pivotal moment arrived. A total solar eclipse would be visible in Chile's prime Atacama Desert. This was a perfect chance to test and show the impact of our storytelling.

As the three years elapsed, it became evident that a powerful new perception had emerged. Astronomy had become one of Chile's most recognized attributes on the global stage. Its visibility had grown a lot. It became an official pillar, integrated into the country's brand.

The campaign caused a surge in foreign tourists. It sparked a wave of local media coverage. The coverage focused on astronomy and astro-tourism. The eclipse happened in a remote place on a weekday. Despite this, over 300,000 people flocked to the Atacama Desert to see it. We had

---

80 Thanks to its geography and areas with low population density, Chile is home to the darkest skies in the world, with zero or extremely low light pollution, and with a higher percentage of clear nights per year on the planet. This is the case of Cerro Armazones, with an average of 330 nights a year (89%), compared to Hawaii and the Canary Islands, 76% and 73%, respectively. The observatories are located in places where skies have the greatest atmospheric stability in the world (seeing), reaching values as low as 0.3 arc-seconds, while in places such as the Canary Islands or Hawaii, the average is 0.75 arc-seconds. They also have the lowest humidity values in the world and electromagnetic interference so low that it is only comparable to Antarctica. (Cavazzani et al., 2011; Hickson, 2010; Thomas-Osip et al., 2011). Currently, a third of the observation capacity (collection area) of the world's infrared and optical telescopes is installed in Chile, and it is estimated that it will reach 70% by 2025. Also, during the day, the North of Chile and in particular the Atacama Desert, is the place of the earth that receives the largest solar radiation in the world, with a potential installed capacity of solar energy around 200,000MW, equivalent to 30 % of South America's electricity consumption in 2030. (SERC, 2014).

already noticed a big rise in public interest. This was shown in more media coverage. But the rise that day was far bigger.

Reaching the eclipse viewing area required a 400-kilometer journey north. It crossed the southern edges of the desert. The normally quiet roads now were full of cars. A relentless influx of visitors overflowed gas stations and local businesses. On a normal holiday, these traffic jams would annoy people. This is especially true for those behind the wheel. But now, the atmosphere was very festive.

After two and a half hours of driving, the landscape changed. The hills have stunted plants. They turned into the stark, mineral Atacama Mountains. I remembered a talk I had with Demetrio, a French engineer and photography fan. He works at Paranal, a site of the European Southern Observatory (ESO). He was an ardent admirer of the desert's unique character. He explained to me that the Atacama Desert is unlike other top spots for astronomy. It lacks plants and has no volcanoes. "It's like Mars," he said. "In the days with no wind, you can have absolute silence. If you stand still, you then hear your own heartbeats and nothing else. There are very few places on Earth where you can experience that."

As we approached the area we were heading, we saw more people. They were going into the dry hills to secure their viewing spots. We were joined by three other couples, each with their children. Upon reaching our base camp, we wasted no time in setting up a barbecue. The mood was friendly and supportive. It wasn't long before we were sharing drinks with our neighbors.

The moment the moon began to cover the sun, an ethereal, almost ghostly shadow fell on everything. It was an alien spectacle unlike anything I had ever witnessed. The world seemed to slow down as the shadows muted the surroundings. My wife, friends, and children were a captivating blend of awe, wonder, and pure joy. It was one of the best experiences of my life.

Back in the city, our team worked on the astronomy project. We got together to comment on the eclipse and review its impact. We were very pleased. The media coverage far exceeded our expectations. In almost every report, we encountered the key facts and messages we had crafted.

I watched the eclipse with my family and friends. It was one of my dearest personal highlights. It was also a testament to the power of strategic messaging. It can transform things. Here, in the vast Atacama, I saw the huge impact that well-crafted messaging can have. It affects and mobilizes not just individuals, but also groups, organizations, and nations.

Our messaging had a narrative. It was not just words; it was a catalyst for change. It helped Chile become a global leader in astronomy and stargazing. It did this by turning a natural event into a national celebration and economic success. The story we told wasn't just about the stars. It was about the power of talk to show a nation's potential and inspire wonder. It drew the world' eyes to its unique stars.

PART III:

THE MATERIAL

INSTRUCTIVE MANUAL

Step 1: Think first, the plan

Mind the context: I work for the country's leading beverage company (alcoholic and non-alcoholic), with over 5,000 employees and operations across the continent. Five years ago, a percentage of the company was acquired by a multinational brewing company, which owns more than 165 breweries in more than 70 countries. This prompted a new modernization of all processes and the entry of a new management team. I came in with Rosaline, the human resources and organizational development manager, for whom I have become a right-hand man and most trusted advisor.

However, despite the modernization, the company is still traditional in some respects, such as overemphasizing operations and sales to the detriment of other areas. Human resources, for example, has been unable to implement the initiatives in its plans because it encounters indifference or opposition from the sales manager, Ugolino. While very competent, Ugolino is old-fashioned: he considers human resources a service area, not central to the business. Because of the ascendancy of sales in the company, this attitude rubs off on other managers. This hinders alignment and undermines our ethos towards them and the CEO.

Define an outcome that serves your goal: Now, to continue growing in the company and take on a new challenge, I want to move from human resources to sales, which could be done if I apply for a vacancy that has opened in the sales team's management. As I have a commercial profile and experience, together with outstanding results in my current job in human resources, I am an ideal candidate for that position. However, I need the ok of Rosaline, my direct boss. Therefore, I need to ask for her support in a meeting, which will result in her authorizing my application for the sales team job.

COMMUNICATIONAL (outcome)	STRATEGIC (goal)
My boss to authorize my application to the sales team.	Move from HR to Sales

Recognize your Ethos: High regarding both competence and trust. I am second in command, my boss's right-hand man and her most trusted advisor. However, this can play against my plans, as my boss would prefer to retain me at her side and in the HR team.

Know your audience. My boss, Rosaline. She is interested in positioning the HR and OD area as value generator and key contributor to the business (Ebit,) by making it most visible among her peers and showing herself as leader in the eyes of the CEO.

Step 2: Find the hinges: target action and key motivation.

'As a Human Resources and Organizational Development manager of a large company, Rosaline has the following objective *interests* (KPIs): productivity, employee satisfaction, talent recruitment, absenteeism, accident rate, union relations, work climate and engagement.

As for her personal *needs* (individual aims or pain points), one of the most important and urgent is to stop being ignored by Sales. If we get them on board, we can better align the entire management team and, thus, the whole company.

		SEMANTIC HINGES		
Conditions to comply		Outcome's Target action	Audience's Key motivation	Conditions to comply
Executed by the audience.	✓	For my boss to say ok to endorse my application.	Stop being ignored and downgraded by sales.	✓	Traction to my outcome
It occurs on the spot.	✓			✓	Supported by evidence
It is observable.	✓			✓	Relevant to the audience

To endorse my application [verb] stop being ignored by sales

Step 3: Do the magic.

Set the blocks and build the message using an SMM© equation.

SMM© EQUATION = f (X, Y, Z)		
Elements	**Question**	**Result**
X = Audience Y = Audience's Key Motivation Z = Outcome's Target Action	What do I tell an audience X, whose motivation is Y, to make them do Z?	What do I tell my boss Rosaline, whose motivation is stop being ignored by sales, to make her ok to endorse me?

EQUATION > QUESTION				RESULT > MESSAGE		
What do I tell [audience X]	...who want/s to [motivation Y]	...to make them do [outcome Z]	=	Comm. outcome's target action	Verb	Audience's key motivation
Rosaline, my direct boss.	Stop being ignored	Say ok to endorse my application	=	to endorse my application	will help	Stop being ignored

CHOSE DIRECTION (BENEFIT OR HARM)			
SUBJECT	**VERB**	**OBJECT**	**SENSE**
To endorse my application to the sales position	[verb]	Stop being ignored by sales	Obtaining a benefit
		Get the sales team on board	Avoiding harm

To endorse my application **will help** getting the sales team on b|

SUBJECT	VERB		OBJECT	MODE
To endorse my application to the sales position	will (1) (2) would (3) may (4) could (5)	help	Get the sales team on board	(1) *Future indicative* (2) *Present indicative* (3) *Conditional* (4) *Modal verb "may"* (5) *Modal verb "could"*

Step 4: Bring that support

Provide supporting evidence and then calibrate the message according to ethos and evidence.

Having me on the sales team is a unique opportunity to get them on board

As never before, you would have one of your own –me– in a position of influence at the core management of the sales team

Step 5: Making it real

Finish the speech and choose the best order of execution.

MESSAGING SPEECH	⟶	EXECUTION SCRIPT
1. Having me on the sales team is a unique opportunity to get them on board. [message]	[ethos]	1. You know I'm on the same page as you and share your crusade for HR recognition and positioning.
2. As never before, you would have one of your own -me- in a position of influence at the core management of the sales team. [evidence]	[evidence]	2. As never before, you would have one of your own -me- in a position of influence at the core management of the sales team.
3. You know I'm on the same page as you and share your crusade for HR recognition and positioning. [ethos]	[message]	3. Having me on the sales team is a unique opportunity to get them on board.

Execution Script: Hello boss… [greeting-icebreaker]

You know I'm on the same page as you and share your crusade for HR recognition and positioning. [credentials, ethos, talk]

As never before, you would have one of your own -me- in a position of influence at the core management of the sales team. [+ evidence]

Having me on the sales team is a unique opportunity to get them on board.

GLOSSARY
OF TERMS AND DEFINITIONS

Assertion: In linguistics, an assertion is a speech act used to convey and present information as true. It's the act of committing yourself to the truth of a proposition. Therefore, it has a truth-value, which means it is either true or false. For example, "The assertion that the Earth is flat is demonstrably false."

Conjugated verb: It is a verb that has been modified from its base form to show specific grammatical information. This information typically includes person (who is performing the action—I, you, he/she/it, we, they), number (how many are performing the action—singular or plural) and tense (when the action is happening—past, present, future).

Complement (in grammar): a word or group of words that completes the meaning of a sentence, particularly the predicate (verb phrase). There are two main types. (1) Object Complement, which renames, describes, or completes the meaning of the direct or indirect object. For instance, "They elected her president" (President describes "her"). And (2) Subject Complement, which follows a linking verb (like "be," "seem," "become") and provides information about the subject. Example: The house looks beautiful (Beautiful describes the house).

Doxa: commonly translated (from the Greek δόξα) as "opinion," "belief," or "common sense." It refers to generally held beliefs or opinions. Usually based on personal experience, tradition, or what others say, these opinions can be widely shared and influential. However, they may or may not be true as often; although not necessarily false, they are not well-founded.

Episteme: commonly translated as "knowledge" or "scientific knowledge," it refers to justified true belief obtained through reason, evidence, and critical thinking. It's a higher level of knowledge that goes beyond mere opinion. Usually, this implies being supported by evidence and reasoning or reached through a rigorous inquiry process.

Ethos: the speaker's credibility and how they establish their trustworthiness or authority on a topic. It's about convincing the audience that you are a credible source and that your perspective deserves to be heard. The source of credibility usually varies according to the audience and can be influenced by the speaker's speech or logos.

Evidence: refers to information used to demonstrate the truth, validity, or likelihood of something. It is usually presented in the form of data, facts, testimonies, or documents and used to build a case for a particular conclusion (although it doesn't guarantee absolute truth). The strength of evidence is variable and depends on its relevance, reliability, and sufficiency.

Fact: is an objective statement about something known to be true or has been proven true. It must be objective and verifiable. A fact is independent of opinion (not based on personal beliefs or feelings) and can be checked and confirmed through evidence or established knowledge.

Goal: It's something you strive for and aim to accomplish within a specific timeframe, usually involving intermediate steps when the goal is strategic.

It refers to a desired result that a person or group envisions, plans, and commits to achieving. In this book, the term refers specifically to the (strategic) end goal, which is the destination of a plan and its strategic streamline. Nothing comes afterwards; it's the result.

Interest: refers to an objective (extrinsic) motivation a person or a group may have, usually an imposed constraint or an external outcome. Interests are role-determined and mappable to a person's position, profile, or occupation. Because they are concrete, interests are usually expressed in quantifiable units. Therefore, they often coincide with key performance indicators (KPIs).

Judgement: is a speech act that uses language to evaluate something and express an opinion or belief about it. It's a way of conveying your assessment and potentially influencing the way others perceive the subject. As interpretations and points of view, they are never true or false but well-founded or poorly founded. This support is done by assertions and separate and complementary speech acts.

Key Motivation: an audience's motivation that serves the purpose of being incorporated into the message as persuasive leverage. To be persuasive, it should meet three conditions: It must be relevant to the audience, have traction aligned with my outcome, and seem possible when added to the message.

Logos: a Greek word (λόγος) that combines and integrates two meanings: language, word, and speech; and thought and reason. In philosophy, rhetoric, and psychology, logos refers to using logic and reason in communication or persuasion. It's about using evidence and arguments to convince someone of something.

Message: a communication that conveys information between a sender and a receiver. It can be delivered in many ways, including verbally, written, visually, or even through the content of a piece of art, which can all be considered messages. The message can contain information, instructions, ideas, or emotions.

Motivation: is the internal and external factors that inspire, direct, and encourage someone to act. It can be driven by needs, desires, goals, or rewards. They are categorized in two types: interests and needs.

Need: it refers to a particular person's or group's longing or pain point. In contrast to interests, which tend to be extrinsic and objective, needs are subjective and specific. They can be extrinsic and intrinsic —the motivation to do something for its own sake or enjoyment.

Objective: a measurable goal or a step towards achieving another outcome within a defined stream of actions and tasks. Most long-term plans include intermediate steps or milestones to accomplish. They are commonly referred to as "tactical" objectives.

Outcome: The outcome should be understood and defined as what you get when achieving the objective. The first is the goal of the individual communication act —the conversation, meeting, or presentation. That will be the "outcome".

Pathos: refers to an appeal to an audience's emotions. It's a persuasive technique used in writing, speeches, and other communications to evoke feelings and connect on an emotional level. The goal is to use those emotions to influence the audience's opinion or behavior. It is one of three components of rhetoric, along with ethos and logos.

Reference: the connection between words or expressions and the things in the world they point to. This could be physical objects, ideas, concepts, or even other words, concepts, or mental objects. Some philosophers distinguish between a word's reference (the thing it points to) and its sense (the concept or idea associated with the word). For instance, the words "morning star" and "evening star" both refer to the planet Venus but have different senses.

Slogan: it is a memorable phrase or motto used to convey information in a short, catchy way. It's often used in advertising, marketing, and political campaigns to promote a product, service, or cause, create brand identity, persuade, or influence. They are usually memorable, clear, concise, benefit-oriented, and unique (to stand out from the competition.)

Speech Act: this is a way of understanding communication beyond simply saying something. It focuses on the utterance's action rather than just the information it conveys. Along with the actual saying or signing of the words or message, it also considers the speaker's intention (he or she might want to inform, request, warn, apologize or promise) and the effect on the listener. This could be understanding new information, acting, feeling a certain way, or changing.

Strategy: a plan to achieve a mid-to-long term goal under conditions of uncertainty. It's essentially a roadmap that outlines how to get from where you are to where you want to be. A strategy always focuses on achieving specific goals, whether winning a competition, growing a business, or completing a project. It is typically concerned with long-term objectives (rather than short-term wins), considers the future as inherently uncertain and, as such, involves making decisions about how to allocate resources (time, money, people, etc.) and adapt to changing circumstances to achieve the goals.

Target action: A well-formulated communicational outcome must meet three conditions. First, it must prompt the audience to act. That action from the audience's side must occur at the exact moment (ipso facto, not ex-post.)

Techne: is a concept in ancient Greek philosophy that refers to making or doing. It encompasses a broad range of activities that involve applying knowledge and skill to achieve a desired outcome -from crafting furniture to performing surgery. Techne also refers to specific expertise or knowledge in a particular domain, like medicine or rhetoric, as well as to creations, whether it's a physical object, a piece of art, or even knowledge itself.

Truth: the correspondence of language or thought to a mind-independent world. In everyday language, this is defined as being correspondent to facts or reality.

Veracity: refers to the quality of being truthful or accurate. It could refer to someone's general disposition to tell the truth and be honest (habitual truthfulness) and, therefore, can be relied upon to give accurate information or to the accuracy of statements or information (conformity to truth). Here, veracity focuses on the content itself, whether it corresponds to reality or not. A news report has veracity if the information it presents is factually correct.

REFERENCES

Albertus, M. & V. Menaldo. (2018). *Authoritarianism and the Elite Origins of Democracy*. Cambridge: Cambridge University 9Press.

America Succeeds, EMSI, Burning Glass (2021). *The High Demand for Durable Skills*. https://americasucceeds.org/portfolio/the-high-demand-for-durable-skills-october-2021

Arendt, H. (2017). *Verdad y mentira en la política*. Barcelona: Página Indómita.

Aristotle (1990). *Retórica*. Madrid: Editorial Gredos.

Austin, J. (1962). *How to do Things with Words*. Oxford: Clarendon Press.

Bartlett, R. C. (2019). *Aristotle's Art of Rhetoric*. Chicago: The University of Chicago Press.

Bauman, Z. (2000). *Liquid Modernity*. Cambridge, England: Polity Press.

Baggini, J. (2018). *How the World Thinks*. London: Granta Books.

Beckett, A. (2003). *Pinochet in Piccadilly*. London: Faber and Faber.

Benjamin, S. (1997). *Words at Work: Business Writing in Half the Time with Twice the Power*. New York: Basic Books.

Berman, M. (1983). *All that Is Solid Melts into the Air: The Experience of Modernity.* New York: Verso.

Biehl, A. & Vera, G. (2013). *Contra la Libertad.* Santiago de Chile: Editorial Ariel.

Birchard, B. (2021). 'The Science of Strong Business Writing.' *Harvard Business Review.* July 2021.

Bloom, P. (2021). *Lo que está en juego.* Madrid: Anagrama.

Bloom, P. (2010). *The Vertigo Years: Europe, 1900-1914.* New York: Basic Books.

Bostock, D. (1988). *Plato's Theaetetus.* Oxford: Oxford University Press

Brouk, T. (2018). 'To Give a Great Presentation, Distil your Message into Just 15 Words.' *Harvard Business Review*, November 2018.

Bruner, J. (1991). 'The narrative construction of reality.' *Critical Inquiry*, 18: pp. 1–21.

Case, A. & A. Deaton (2015). 'Rising Morbidity and Mortality in Midlife among White Non-Hispanic Americans in the 21st Century.' *Proceedings of the National Academy of Science.* Vol. 112, No. 49, pp. 15078-15083.

Castells, M. (2009). *Comunicación y poder.* Madrid: Alianza Editorial.

Cialdini, R. (2007). *Influence: The Psychology of Persuasion.* New York: Harper Collins Business Essentials.

Cialdini, R. (2001). 'Harnessing the Science of Persuasion.' *Harvard Business Review.* October 2001.

CNBC (2018). 'Billionaire Warren Buffett: This is the 'one easy way' to increase your worth by at least' 50 per cent. https://www.cnbc.com/2018/12/05/warren-buffett-how-to-increase-your-worth-by-50-percent.html.

Clark, R. P. (2006). *Writing Tools*. New York: Little Brown Books.

Crossman, R. H. (2017). *Plato Today*. London: Routledge.

Davidson, D., (1979). 'Moods and performances,' reprinted in Davidson (1984) *Inquiries into Truth and Interpretation*. Oxford: Oxford University Press.

Deenan, P. (2018). *Why Liberalism Failed*. New Haven: Yale University Press.

Denton, R. E. Jr. (1980). "The Rhetorical Function of Slogans: Classification and Characteristics." *Communication Quarterly*. 28 (2): 10–18.

Duarte, N. (2008). *Slide:ology: The Art and Science of Creating Great Presentations*. O'Reilly.

Dunbar, R. (1998). 'The Social Brain Hypothesis'. *Evolutionary Anthropology*. Vol. 6, Issue 5, pp. 178-190.

Eemeren, F.H. van & Grootendorst, R. & Jackson, S. & Jacobs, S. (1997). 'Argumentación.' En: Van Dijk, T.A. (ed.). *El discurso como estructura y proceso* (vol. 1). Barcelona: Gedisa

Fortenbaugh, R. (1975). *Aristotle on Emotion: A Contribution to Philosophical Psychology, Rhetoric, Poetics, Politics and Ethics*. London: Duckworth.

Foster Wallace, D. (1997) 'E Unibus Pluram.' In *A Supposedly Fun Thing I'll Never Do Again: Essays and Arguments*. Boston: Little Brown & Co.

Forrester, J. (2013). *Industrial Dynamics*. Eastford, CT: Martino Fine Books.

Field, G.C. (1967). *Plato and his Contemporaries*. Methuen & Co; New Ed edition.

Fukuyama (2008): 'The End of America Inc.' *Newsweek*. October 4, 2008. Retrieved October 24, 2008, www.newsweek.com.

Godin, S. (2001) *Really Bad PowerPoint*. Seth's Blog. https://seths.blog/2007/01/really_bad_powe/

Green, R. (2008). *The 48 Laws of Power*. London: Profile Books.

Guthrie, W. K. C. (1979). *A History of Greek Philosophy: Volume 4, Plato: The Man and his Dialogues: Earlier Period (Plato - The Man & His Dialogues - Earlier Period)*. Cambridge University Press.

Hallsworth, M. & E. Kirkman (2020*). Behavioral Insights*. Cambridge, Massachusetts: The MIT Press.

Harari, Y. (2008*). Sapiens: A Brief History of Humankind*. Harper Perennial.

Harvey, D. (2005*). A Brief History of Neoliberalism*. Oxford: Oxford University Press.

Heath, C & D. Heath (2007). *Made to Stick: Why Some Ideas Survive, and Others Die*. New York Random House.

Hofstede, G. (2010). *Cultures and Organizations: Software of the Mind*. New York: McGraw Hill.

Hunt, A. (2008). *Pragmatic Thinking & Learning*. The Pragmatic Programmers.

Johnstone, P. & C. McLeish (2020). 'World Wars and The Age of Oil: Exploring Directionality in Deep Energy Transitions' in *Energy Research & Social Science*. Vol 69: November 2020, 101732.

Jones, R.; Cox D. & R. Lienesch (2017). 'Beyond Economics: Fears of Cultural Displacement Pushed the White Working Class to Trump' PRRI/*The Atlantic Report*. PRI.

Kahneman, D. (2011). *Thinking Fast and Slow*. New York: Farrar, Strauss and Giroux.

Kress, G. (2005). *El alfabetismo en la era de los nuevos medios de comunicación*. Granada: Enseñanza Abierta.

Lakoff, G., and M. Johnson (1980). *Metaphors We Live By*. Chicago: University of Chicago Press.

Lockwood, T. (1996). *The Reader's Figure: Epideictic Rhetoric in Plato, Aristotle, Bossuet, Racine and Pascal*. Geneva: Librairie Droz.

Luntz, F. (2007). *Words at Work*. New York: Hyperion Books.

McCreadie, K. (2018). *Sun Tzu's The Art of War: A 52 Brilliant Ideas Interpretation*. Infinite Ideas.

McKeown, M. (2015). *The Strategy Book: How to think and act strategically to deliver outstanding results*. London: FT Press.

McLuhan, M. (1996). *Understanding Media: The Extensions of Man*. Boston: MIT University Press.

Moreno, F. (2008). Silent Revolution: An Early Export from Pinochet's Chile. "*Journal Of Globalization, Competitiveness, And Governability*." Georgetown University Vol. 2, No. 2.

Most, W. G. (1994) 'The Uses of Endoxa.' In *Aristotle's Rhetoric*. Princeton University Press.

Motesharrei, S.; Rivas, J. y E. Kalnay (2014). 'Human and Nature Dynamics (HANDY): Modeling Inequality and Resource Use in the Collapse or Sustainability of Societies.' *Ecological Economics*. Vol 101, pp 90 -102.

Naím, M. (2016). *El Fin del Poder*. Madrid: Debate.

Nehamas, A. (1994). 'The Rhetoric and the Poetics' in *Aristotle's Rhetoric*. Princeton University Press.

Patterson, K et al. (2002). *Crucial Conversations: Tools for Talking When Stakes are High*. McGraw-Hill.

Pettegree, A. (2014). *The Invention of News: How the World Came to Know About Itself*. New Haven and London: Yale University Press.

Plato (2003). *Diálogos*. Volumen I, II, IV. Madrid: Gredos.

Politico (2015). 'The ten best lines from Donald Trump's announcement speech.' In *Politico*. Retrieved on 06/16/2015. https://www.politico.com/story/2015/06/donald-trump-2016-announcement-10-best-lines-119066.

Rodríguez-Adrados, F. (1997). *Democracia y literatura en la Atenas clásica*. Madrid: Alianza.

Sapolsky, M. (2017). *Behave: The Biology of Humans at Our Best and Worst*. New York: Penguin Books.

Scruton, R. (1996). *Modern Philosophy: An Introduction and Survey*. London: Penguin.

Searle, J. R. (1969). *Speech Acts*. Cambridge: Cambridge University Press.

Smil, V. (2022). *How the Word Really Works: The Science Behind How We Got Here and Where We're Going*. London: Viking.

Society for Human Resources Management (2019). *The Global Skills Shortage: Bridging the Talent Gap with Education, Training and Sourcing*. SHRM.

Stanford Encyclopaedia of Philosophy, 2018. The Definition of Art. https://plato.stanford.edu/entries/art-definition/index.html#ref-1

Sterman, J. (2000). *Business Dynamics: Systems Thinking and Modelling for a Complex World*. Boston: Irwin McGraw-Hill.

Stevenson, A. (2010). Oxford Dictionary of English (Vol. III). Oxford University Press. doi:10.1093/acref/9780199571123.001.0001. ISBN 978-0199571123.

Suarez, M. (Ed.). (2004). *Just a few sayings...I made up*. Wendell: The Virginia Satir Global Network.

Taleb, N. (2012). *Antifragile: Things that Gain from Disorder*. New York: Random House.

The Daily Mail (2016). 'Enemies of the People.' https://www.dailymail.co.uk/news/article-3903436/Enemies-people-Fury-touch-judges-defied-17-4m-Brexit-voters-trigger-constitutional-crisis.html.

The Economist (2015). 'Men Adrift. Badly educated men in rich countries have not adapted well to trade, technology or feminism.' https://www.economist.com/essay/2015/05/28/men-adrift.

Thompson, M. (2017). *Enough Said: What's Gone Wrong with the Language of Politics.* New York: St. Martin's Press.

Van Steen, E. (2021). 'Strategy and strategic thinking.' *Harvard Business Review.* March, 721-431.

Veyne P. (2009). *El imperio grecorromano.* Ediciones Akal: Madrid.

Weick, K. E. (1995). 'Sensemaking in Organizations.' *In Foundations for Organizational Science.* London: Sage Publications.

Wreden, N. (2009). 'How to make your case in 30 seconds or less.' *Harvard Business Review,* January 2002.

Zeihan, P. (2022). *The end of the world is just the beginning: Mapping the collapse of globalization.* New York: Harper Business.

Zinsser, W. (2006). *On Writing Well.* New York: Quill Harper Resource Books.

Made in United States
Cleveland, OH
29 October 2024

10356738R00125